T0266174

Leon Trotsky and the
Organizational Principles
of the Revolutionary Party

Leon Trotsky and the Organizational Principles of the Revolutionary Party

Dianne Feeley, Paul Le Blanc, and Thomas Twiss

International Socialism Series
Haymarket Books
Chicago, Illinois

© 2014 Dianne Feeley, Paul Le Blanc, and Thomas Twiss

Published in 2014 by
Haymarket Books
P.O. Box 180165
Chicago, IL 60618
773-583-7884
info@haymarketbooks.org
www.haymarketbooks.org

ISBN: 978-1-60846-396-1

Trade distribution:
In the US, Consortium Book Sales and Distribution, www.cbsd.com
In Canada, Publishers Group Canada, www.pgcbooks.ca
In the UK, Turnaround Publisher Services, www.turnaround-uk.com
All other countries, Ingram Publisher Services International, ips_intlsales@
ingramcontent.com

Special discounts are available for bulk purchases by organizations
and institutions. Please contact Haymarket Books for more information
at 773-583-7884 or info@haymarketbooks.org.

Cover design by Josh On.

Library of Congress CIP data is available.

Entered into digital printing June 2018.

CONTENTS

Chapter 3

Toward the World Party of Socialist Revolution 41

Prefatory note from the authors

This is a compilation, produced more than a quarter of a century ago, from the writings of Leon Trotsky. It is a survey of ways that Trotsky understood the organizational perspectives associated with a distinctively revolutionary current that arose in the Russian socialist movement, the Bolsheviks, under the leadership of Vladimir Ilyich Lenin. It also gives a sense of how Trotsky sought to apply those perspectives to complex and shifting realities, from the Russian Revolution of 1917 down to the year of his death in 1940.

We want to convey to the reader of today the 1982 context in which we produced this document. At the time, there was a political crisis developing in a U.S. revolutionary organization to which we had committed our lives, the Socialist Workers Party. Dianne had joined in 1967. Paul joined the Young Socialist Alliance (YSA), the party youth group in 1972, and the SWP a year later, Tom joined the YSA in 1973 and the SWP in 1976. We were proud of the SWP's revolutionary Marxist traditions, its deep roots in what we felt was the best in the history of U.S. radicalism, and especially in the struggles of our own time—against the Vietnam war, against racism, for women's liberation, for gay and lesbian rights, in opposition to the environmental degradation of our planet, and especially for the struggles of the working-class majority to defend its living and working conditions and—eventually—to place the economic resources and institutions of society under the democratic control of its people. We were proud of the role played by the early leaders of the SWP—people like James P. Cannon, Rose Karsner, Vincent Raymond Dunne, Antoinette Konikow, Farrell Dobbs, Joe Hansen, George Breitman, and others—in the struggles of the working class during the first six decades of the twentieth century. We were inspired that a transition was taking place in the 1970s to a younger leadership layer, whose central figure was part of our own generation, Jack Barnes.

With the end of the Vietnam war, however, it was not clear what the SWP might continue to do that would enable it to play a leadership role in other mass movements. Nor was it clear what "mass movements" might be in the offing. A decision to break up large branches in order to establish smaller "community branches" turned out to be an unmitigated flop. A "turn to the working class"—getting more and more comrades into union jobs, especially in industrial occupations—seemed promising to many of us, but certainly did not replicate the impact on political realities that the SWP had appeared to enjoy in the earlier anti-war movement. This seemed to be contrary to the expectation that the 1960s radicalization among students and youth would inexorably embrace the entire working class in the 1970s and 1980s.

After a brief period of apparent uncertainty, the new leadership embarked on a dramatic new course—although Barnes and his co-thinkers were carrying this out in the name of "revolutionary continuity." Nonetheless, Barnes and those around him were quietly but increasingly distancing themselves from the traditional Trotskyist perspectives that had guided the SWP, replacing that with an uncritical attitude toward the leadership of the Cuban Communist Party led by Fidel Castro. An internal educational campaign was initiated to read Lenin—and to read Lenin in the "correct" way—in order to achieve a correct political orientation consistent with the shift away from Trotsky. And in the name of "Leninism" and "democratic centralism," the new leadership was also suppressing internal democracy.

Although it did not occur to us at the time, it seems that it was important to those in the Barnes leadership that they remain in leadership positions no matter what—which required that they tighten up the organizational norms more than ever, because some of their comrades might question what appeared to be a certain amount of political flailing about. Some would certainly not go along with their junking of the old concepts that had guided the organization.

Even before the early 1980s, when this development transformed the SWP, we had been taught to accept a more restrictive understanding of "Leninist norms" than any of us would accept today. Uncomfortable with increasing organizational restrictions in the late 1960s, the retired leader of U.S. Trotskyism, James P. Cannon, had warned: "don't strangle the party" in a communication to the SWP leadership, but was basically ignored. In a factional dispute in the mid-1970s, party norms had been further tightened when a dissident current was "de-registered"—which amounted to being thrown out of the SWP without a trial. But now the SWP's political line could change overnight, with few daring to question these changes—in regard to such things as the Russian invasion of Afghanistan, or the Polish workers struggling for their rights, or the increasingly draconian pressures to force all SWP members into industrial jobs, while abandoning a variety of social movements, pulling out of union jobs among teachers and service workers, etc. This intensified "industrialization" policy (referred to as "the turn within the turn") was also forced on the Young Socialist Alliance, with the motivation that the student movement was dead—although in reality the student movement was building anti-divestment campaigns on the campuses against South African apartheid, involving itself in Central America solidarity efforts, and pushing against cut-backs and tuition hikes.

Barnes loyalists were becoming increasingly aggressive in party branches such as ours in Pittsburgh. Those of us who clearly disagreed with what was happening had to watch our step, and we were removed from all but the most limited internal assignments, watched closely by the "loyalists" who were on the lookout for disciplinary infractions. Party norms began to generate an atmosphere that felt claustrophobic and cold—it was like living in a refrigerator—with a growing number of our comrades afraid to talk with us when we even timidly raised questions or made suggestions about areas of work where we might work with other leftists. But the hard "loyalists" didn't seem to be afraid, and explained behind our backs as well as at branch meetings that not only were we wrong, but we were "bourgeois intellectuals" with "no roots in the working class."

Actually, the three of us were from working-class families and supported ourselves proletarian-style by selling our ability to work for a paycheck. We were part of a current in the SWP that was committed to having a full-scale democratic discussion—in order to struggle for a more honest and open way of functioning, consistent with the Trotskyist perspectives to which we had been recruited in the 1960s and 1970s. We wanted to stay in the party in order to fight for its future as a revolutionary force, hopefully by waking up our comrades and winning them to our ideas. According to the SWP constitution, there was supposed to be a pre-convention discussion in the months leading up to the 1983 national convention, with written documents to be published in pre-convention discussion bulletins as well as organized branch discussions. At the request of George Breitman (1916-1986), we agreed to prepare "Leon Trotsky and the Organizational Principles of the Revolutionary Party" in 1982. He proposed that it be prepared for the SWP's National Education Department as an educational bulletin—and, if it was ignored or rejected (it was ignored), it could be one of the documents that would be printed in the pre-convention discussion bulletins. (Another piece of writing produced under Breitman's influence at this time was Paul Le Blanc's book *Lenin and the Revolutionary Party*.)

We felt honored to be collaborating with Breitman. He was best known as a meticulous editor of the influential volume *Malcolm X Speaks* and the fourteen-volume *Writings of Leon Trotsky, 1929-1940*. But he also had a reputation as an experienced party cadre, active since the early 1930s, with a critical and creative intelligence, a person of integrity, and a leader in opposing the abandonment of Trotskyism and of the undemocratic developments being advanced in the name of "Leninism."

As the three of us worked together on this document, we ourselves were looking for answers, and as we combed through Trotsky's writings, we found that his views were quite different from what we were experiencing in the SWP. It was an exhilarating experience, and we were excited with the prospect of presenting this to our comrades in the SWP's pre-convention discussion. But instead the Barnes leadership cancelled the national convention. Dianne and then Paul were brought up on charges and expelled; Tom was also brought up on charges, but resigned before his scheduled trial and expulsion. Two hundred people were expelled in this period, hundreds of others left, and in the succeeding years the SWP deteriorated into an ingrown sect.

After his own expulsion, Breitman became a leader of the Fourth Internationalist Tendency (the FIT), a small group which existed from 1984 to 1993, publishing this document in its first year of existence. For aspects of this group's history and perspectives, and its account of the degeneration of the SWP, see the section on the Fourth Internationalist Tendency in the Encyclopedia of Trotskyism on Line, contained within the Marxist Internet Archive: http://www.marxists.org/history/etol/document/fit.htm.

While Paul joined the FIT, Tom and Dianne joined Solidarity. Later, when the FIT dissolved, Paul joined too. At present Dianne is a member of Solidarity and an editor of *Against the Current*, Tom is politically independent, and Paul is a member of the International Socialist Organization. Each of us has remained true to basic revolutionary socialist beliefs, and each has sought to contribute something to the socialist and labor movements. With the passage of time, however, the thinking of each has continued to evolve. We do not fully agree with each other on all matters, nor do we all share the same views on the value or relevance of Leninist-Trotskyist perspectives on organization. We have taken the liberty of making a number of relatively modest editorial revisions, especially in the final section of chapter 3, part 5 (the nature of some of these changes being reflected in the title change of that section from "The Petty Bourgeois Opposition" to "The 1939-40 Factional Dispute"). The basic political content of the document has not been altered, however.

Serious Marxists are never content to settle issues simply by referring to quotes from historic figures. Texts must be critically related to the contexts in which they were expressed, and the differences (as well as similarities) between bygone contexts and our own time must also be considered. No compendium of quotations can be seen as the "last word" on any subject. Nonetheless, we believe that both scholars and activists may find this to be a useful contribution to their thinking.

Introductory note George Breitman, November 1984

This is the first comprehensive examination of Leon Trotsky's views on revolutionary organizational principles and norms from 1917 to 1940. It consists primarily of quotations rather than interpretations and is organized in three sections: 1) a summary of Trotsky's basic conception of organizational principles; 2) an account of Trotsky's defense of Bolshevik norms during the struggle of the Left Opposition in Russia from 1923 to 1929; and 3) a survey of Trotsky's views during the exile of 1929 to 1940, when he led the International Left Opposition and the Fourth International.

Like many other books and pamphlets produced in the Marxist movement, this one resulted from a political struggle. In March 1982 the leadership of the Socialist Workers Party began to gag and threaten members who were opposed to the leadership's moves to revise the party program without membership discussion or approval. The SWP's traditional democratic procedures and safeguards came under attack from the leadership in the form of "new organizational norms."

The present work was written by three members of the Pittsburgh branch of the SWP—Dianne Feeley, Paul Le Blanc, and Thomas Twiss—who submitted it to the SWP's National Educational Department in September 1982 for publication in an educational bulletin. The SWP leadership had no intention of printing anything in such contradiction to the political purge they were conducting. Less than a year later, two of the three authors had been expelled on false and flimsy charges and the third resigned from the SWP in protest. By the start of 1984 the leadership had expelled or driven out hundreds of other members for the crime of defending revolutionary internationalism and democratic centralism. Most of the purged SWP members have appealed their expulsion to the next World Congress of the Fourth International and the struggle to build a mass revolutionary party in this country continues. We [the Fourth Internationalist Tendency] publish this study as a valuable educational weapon in that struggle.

INTRODUCTION

"Renegades are always distinguished by short memories or assume that other people have short memories," wrote Leon Trotsky in 1929. "Revolutionaries, on the contrary, enjoy good memories, which is why it can be truthfully said *the revolutionary party is the memory of the working class.* Learning not to forget the past in order to foresee the future is our first, our most important task." (*Writings, 1929*, p. 202)

For revolutionaries of our time, the views of Trotsky himself on the organizational principles of the revolutionary party are of special importance. The most consistent and profound body of thought relating to such organizational principles can be found in the Bolshevik tradition initiated by V.I. Lenin. This tradition was enriched by Trotsky when he embraced it in 1917: he brought to it the fertile revolutionary experiences of two decades, particularly the perspective of permanent revolution which flowed from the 1905 uprising of the Russian working class. As a Bolshevik leader second only to Lenin, he helped the Bolsheviks lead the workers to power in October/November 1917. From 1919 to 1922, he played a central role in developing and propagating these organizational principles on a world scale through the Communist International. From 1923 onward, he was the foremost opponent of the bureaucratic assaults on, and corruption of, Bolshevik norms perpetrated by Joseph Stalin and his allies. From 1933 until his death in 1940, Trotsky tirelessly labored to establish a new World Party of Socialist Revolution (the Fourth International) that would be infused with the political and organizational principles of Bolshevism. In all of this, the Bolshevik tradition continued to be enriched, and an invaluable reservoir of lessons and insights on the organizational principles of the revolutionary party is consequently available to serious revolutionaries.

The purpose here is to review what Trotsky had to say about the revolutionary party and its organizational principles. This review will consist primarily of quotations rather than interpretations and will be organized into three sections: 1) a summary of Trotsky's basic conception of organizational principles; 2) an examination of Trotsky's defense of Bolshevik norms during the struggle of the Left Opposition in Russia from 1923 to 1929; and 3) an examination of Trotsky's views during the exile of 1929 to 1940, when he led the International Left Opposition and the Fourth International.

The revolutionary party: Its function and its consequent norms

In *The History of the Russian Revolution*, Trotsky discusses "the premises of a revolution": the inability of the existing social structure to solve the country's urgent problems; the resulting loss of faith of the ruling class in itself; the growing militancy and political consciousness of the working class; the intensifying discontent of the broad layers of the petty bourgeoisie. But these factors alone are not sufficient. Trotsky writes:

> The proletariat can become imbued with the confidence necessary for a governmental overthrow only if a clear prospect opens before it, only if it has had an opportunity to test out in action a correlation of forces which is changing to its advantage, only if it feels above it a far-sighted, firm and confident leadership. This brings us to the last premise—by no means the last in importance—of the conquest of power: the revolutionary party as a tightly welded and tempered vanguard of the class.
>
> Thanks to a favorable combination of historic conditions both domestic and international, the Russian proletariat was headed by a party of extraordinary political clarity and unexampled revolutionary temper. Only this permitted that small and young class to carry out a historic task of unprecedented proportions. It is indeed the general testimony of history—the Paris Commune, the German and Austrian revolutions of 1918, the Soviet revolutions in Hungary and Bavaria, the Italian revolution of 1919, the German crisis of 1923, the Chinese revolution of 1925-1927, the Spanish revolution of 1931—that up to now the weakest link in the chain of necessary conditions has been the party. The hardest thing of all is for the working class to create a revolutionary organization capable of

rising to the height of its historic task. (*History of the Russian Revolution*, Vol. III, p. 175)

To understand the problem of creating such a revolutionary organization, one should look at the fate of the pre-World War I German Social Democracy. "For us Russians," Trotsky wrote, "the German Social Democracy was mother, teacher, and living example. We idealized it from a distance." (*My Life*, p. 212) Before the war,

> the Social Democracy built up the unique structure of the political organization of the German proletariat with its many-branched bureaucratic hierarchy, its one million dues-paying members, its four million voters, ninety-one daily papers and sixty-five party printing presses. This whole many-sided activity, of immeasurable historic importance, was permeated through and through with the spirit of possibilism [i.e., of a reformist adaptation to capitalism].

On the theoretical level, this resulted in a fierce dispute between reformists and Marxists.

> Marxism emerged from this theoretical dispute as the victor all along the line. But Revisionism…continued to live, drawing sustenance from the actual conduct and the psychology of the whole movement…. The parliamentarians, the unionists, the comrades continued to live and work in the atmosphere of general opportunism, of practical specializing and of nationalistic narrowness. (*The War and the International*, pp. 58, 60)

As early as 1905, Trotsky had the premonition "That the gigantic machine of the German Social Democracy might, at a critical moment for the bourgeois society, prove to be the mainstay of the conservative order. At the time, however, I did not foresee to what extent this theoretical presumption would be confirmed by the facts." (*My Life*, p. 204)

The First World War and its aftermath provided the most shocking confirmation, when the party's left-wing—seeking to remain true to the revolutionary principles of Marxism—was crushed by a party majority which had adapted only too well to the capitalist environment. While Lenin's illusion in the German Social Democracy had been as great as Trotsky's, his own organizational perspectives for the Russian movement had been far better able to prevent a similar degeneration. He grasped that, as Trotsky later remarked, "a *revolutionary* majority can be won only by a tendency which is capable in the most difficult conditions of remaining true to itself." (*Writings, 1929*, p. 184) This meant not simply refusing to compromise over principles with outright reformists, but also refusing to compromise organizationally with seemingly revolutionary-minded currents that conciliated with reformists. This uncompromising attitude over the party's revolutionary program naturally gave the Bolsheviks the reputation of being "divisive" and "unreasonable," as Trotsky frequently stressed:

> Lenin himself has more than once been accused of having forgotten about and helped the right in his struggle with the left centrists. I myself more than once made such an accusation against Lenin [before 1917]. It is in this, and not at all in permanent revolution, that the basic error of what is called "historical Trotskyism" lay. In order to become a Bolshevik not on a Stalinist passport but in actuality it is necessary to understand fully the meaning and significance of Lenin's irreconcilability toward centrism, without which there is not and cannot be a road to proletarian revolution. (*Writings, 1929*, p. 186)

The essential first principle of Leninist organizational norms is the question of uncompromising political clarity and undeviating adherence to the revolutionary political program. The inseparable link, for Leninists, between the revolutionary program and party organization was explained by Trotsky in this way: "The significance of the program is the significance of the party.... Now, what is the party? In what does the cohesion exist? This cohesion is the common understanding of the events, of the tasks, and this common understanding—this is the program of the party." (*Transitional Program for Socialist Revolution*, p. 136) From this high seriousness over the revolutionary program flows an organizational centralism which is utterly at variance with the seemingly "freer" norms of classical Social Democracy. Trotsky discusses this while describing his own earlier inability to accept Lenin's view on party organization:

> Revolutionary centralism is a harsh, imperative and exacting principle. It often takes the guise of absolute ruthlessness in its relation to individual members, to whole groups of former associates. It is not without significance that the words 'irreconcilable' and 'relentless' are among Lenin's favorites. It is only the most impassioned, revolutionary striving for a definite end—a striving that is utterly free from anything base or personal—that can justify such a personal ruthlessness....
>
> I thought of myself as a centralist. But there is no doubt that at that time I did not fully realize what an intense and imperious centralism the revolutionary party would need to lead millions of people in a war against the old order.... Independently I still could not see Lenin's centralism as the logical conclusion of a clear revolutionary concept. (*My Life*, pp. 161-2)

Trotsky later scoffed at the idealized conception of the Stalinists that "Bolshevism came out of the laboratory of history fully armed," explaining:

> The high temper of the Bolshevik party expressed itself not in an absence of disagreements, waverings, and even quakings, but in the fact that in the most difficult circumstances it gathered itself in good season by means of inner crises, and made good its opportunity to interfere decisively in the course of events. That means that the party as a whole was a quite adequate instrument of revolution. (*My Life*, p. 226; *History*, Vol. III, p. 166)

Through the revolutionary unity of its program, its structure and its norms, the Bolshevik party sought to be an effective instrument of revolution. This instrument would be given life (and would, when necessary, itself be "corrected") by the revolutionaries whose training was the party's primary function.

> Bolshevism created the type of the authentic revolutionist, who subordinates to historic goals irreconcilable with contemporary society the conditions of his personal existence, his ideas, his moral judgments. The necessary distance from bourgeois ideology was kept up in the party by a vigilant irreconcilability, whose inspirer was Lenin. Lenin never tired of working with his lancet, cutting off those bonds which a petty bourgeois environment creates between the party and official social opinion. At the same time Lenin taught the party to create its own social opinion, resting upon the thoughts and feelings of the rising class. Thus by a process of selection and education, and in continual struggle, the Bolshevik party created not only a political but a moral medium of its own, independent of bourgeois social opinion and implacably opposed to it. Only this permitted the Bolsheviks to overcome the waverings in their own ranks and reveal in action that courageous determination without which the October victory would have been impossible. (*History*, Vol. III, p. 166)

This political culture of Bolshevism is based not simply on a revolutionary program, but also, as we have seen, on organizational centralism. But the centralism is, at the same time, necessarily fused with organizational democracy. As Trotsky explains: "The chief aim of the Communist Party is to construct the proletarian vanguard, strongly class-conscious, fit for combat, resolute, prepared for revolution. But revolutionary education requires a regime of internal democracy. Revolutionary discipline has nothing to do with blind obedience." (*Writings*, 1932, p. 326)

The same thought appears in *The History of the Russian Revolution* regarding "how much a revolutionary party has need of internal democracy. The will to struggle is not stored up in advance, and is not dictated from above—it has on every occasion to be independently renewed and tempered." This necessary fusion is reemphasized again and again, as in a declaration written in 1933:

> A supporter of the theory of scientific communism does not take anything on word. He judges everything by reason and experience…. Bureaucratic and artificial discipline has crumbled to dust at the moment of danger. Revolutionary discipline does not exclude but demands the right of checking and criticism. Only in this way can an indestructible revolutionary army be created. (*History*, Vol. III, p. 165; *Writings, 1932-33*, p. 199)

Trotsky stressed that the organizational concepts of "democracy" and "centralism" had no value when abstracted from a revolutionary program for the working class. "Party democracy," he wrote,

> is not necessary in itself but as a means of educating and uniting the proletarian vanguard in the spirit of revolutionary Marxism…. A correct class policy is the main condition for healthy party democracy. Without this, all talk of democracy and discipline remains hollow; worse, it becomes a weapon for the disorganization of the proletarian movement. (*Writings, 1932-33*, p. 88)

It is worth noting that Trotsky did not conceive of "party democracy" as simply an educational device through which the party leadership transmits its political wisdom to the party membership. He stated in 1932, in the case of the Spanish section of the International Left Opposition, that

> subjective arbitrariness in politics would be completely impossible if the Central Committee of the Spanish section worked under the control of their own organization. But this is not the case. In their own defense, several leaders of the Spanish Opposition pointed more than once to the insufficiently high theoretical and political level of the Spanish Oppositionists. Obviously an objection that will not hold water! The level of a revolutionary organization rises all the faster, the more immediately it is brought into the discussion of *all* questions, the less the leaders try to think, act, and behave as guardians for the organization. (*Writings, 1932-33*, p. 26)

Similar distortions of democratic centralism cropped up in other sections of the Opposition as well. For example, problems in the German section in 1931 elicited these comments:

We must not forget that even if we are *centralists*, we are *democratic* centralists who employ centralism only for the revolutionary cause and not in the name of the 'prestige' of the officials. Whoever is acquainted with the history of the Bolshevik Party knows what a broad autonomy the local organizations always enjoyed; they issued their own papers, in which they openly and sharply, whenever they found it necessary, criticized the actions of the Central Committee. Had the Central Committee, in case of principled differences, attempted to disperse the local organizations or to deprive them of literature (their bread and water) before the party had an opportunity to express itself—such a central committee would have made itself impossible. Naturally, as soon as it became necessary, the Bolshevik Central Committee could give orders. BuCt subordination to the committee was possible only because the absolute loyalty of the Central Committee toward every member of the party was well known, as well as the constant readiness of the leadership to hand over every serious dispute for consideration by the party. And, finally, what is most important, the Central Committee possessed extraordinary theoretical and political authority, gained gradually in the course of years, not by commands, not by beating down, but by correct leadership, proved by deeds in great events and struggles. (*Writings, 1930-31,* p. 155)

The inseparable components of Trotsky's basic conception of party organization are: the revolutionary political program of Marxism, organizational centralism, internal democracy. These are the necessary ingredients for a political culture capable of producing an effective revolutionary vanguard of the working class.

The challenge of
the Left Opposition

Chapter 2

"At the moment when it seized the power and created the Soviet republic," wrote Lenin, "Bolshevism drew to itself all the best elements in the currents of Socialist theory that were nearest to it." For example, in September of 1917 the central organ of the Bolsheviks published the words of Trotsky: "A permanent revolution versus a permanent slaughter: that is the struggle, in which the stake is the future of man." (*My Life*, pp. 333, 332) As Trotsky reflected in 1922, his theory of permanent revolution "has been entirely confirmed. The Russian revolution could not culminate in a bourgeois-democratic regime. It had to hand power over to the working class." At the same time that such ideas were being embraced by the Bolsheviks in 1917, Trotsky was won to the Leninist conception of the party, which he came to view as the "fundamental instrument of the proletarian revolution." (*1905*, p. vii; *Challenge of the Left Opposition*, 1926-27, p. 349)

From its earliest years, the internal life of the Bolshevik party had been alive with controversies. "And, indeed," Trotsky later wrote,

> how could a genuinely revolutionary organization, setting itself the task of overthrowing the world and uniting under its banner the most audacious iconoclasts, fighters and insurgents, live and develop without intellectual conflicts, without groupings and temporary factional formations? The farsightedness of the Bolshevik leadership often made it possible to soften conflicts and shorten the duration of the factional struggle, but no more than that. The Central Committee relied upon this seething democratic support. From this it derived the audacity to make decisions and give orders. The obvious correctness of the leadership at all critical stages gave it

that high authority which is the priceless moral capital of centralism. (*The Revolution Betrayed*, p. 95)

Some of the sharpest disputes arose after the Bolshevik seizure of
power, as the revolutionary government faced the gravest problems. During
one of these hotly debated struggles, in January 1921, Lenin voiced concern
that the "fever" of factionalism was becoming "chronic and dangerous." He
was especially concerned about the potential dangers posed by the workerist
and utopian rhetoric of the Workers Opposition. In sharply criticizing this
grouping, however, he continued to support the right of the members to
form inner-party groups that had been respected by the Bolsheviks from
the beginning. "To form ourselves into different groups (especially before a
congress)," Lenin wrote, "is of course permissible (and so is to canvass for
votes). But it must be done within the limits of communism (and not syn-
dicalism) and in such a way as not to provoke laughter." (E.H. Carr, *The Bolshevik Revolution*, Vol. I, p. 204) Expressing the hope that "the Party is
learning not to blow up its disagreements," he approvingly quoted Trotsky's
suggestion that "ideological struggle within the Party does not mean mutual
ostracism but mutual influence." (Lenin, *Selected Works*, Vol. 3, p. 547)

But the picture began to change drastically a few weeks later. In March
1921, the Tenth Congress of the Bolsheviks (now the Communist Party)
was interrupted by the Kronstadt insurrection. Although the Soviet government was able to suppress the uprising, its leaders were deeply dis-
turbed by evidence that the government had lost some of the support it
previously had among the peasant majority of the country. They were also
concerned that the Kronstadt revolt signaled an impending attack by the
imperialist powers. This convinced them that the very future of Soviet
power now depended, above all, on a firm demonstration of unity by the
leaders and members of the Communist Party.

When the Tenth Congress resumed, the Bolsheviks thought it necessary,
for the first time in their eighteen-year history, to ban factions inside the
party. "This forbidding of factions was...regarded as an exceptional measure
to be abandoned at the first serious improvement in the situation," Trotsky
later noted. "At the same time, the Central Committee was extremely cau-
tious in applying the new law, concerning itself most of all lest it lead to a
strangling of the inner life of the party." (*The Revolution Betrayed*, p. 96)

While the Tenth Congress resolution outlawed factional activity, it
clearly did not outlaw democracy. The resolution stated that "criticism of
the party's shortcomings" was "absolutely necessary." It declared that every

practical proposal, "such as purging the Party of non-proletarian and unre-
liable elements, combating bureaucratic practices, developing democracy
and workers' initiative, etc., must be examined with the greatest care and
tested in practice." It pledged the party to "fight with all the means at its
disposal against the evils of bureaucracy" and "for the extension of democracy and initiative." (Lenin, *Selected Works*, Vol. 3, pp. 575-78)

And yet, the difficult circumstances which resulted in this emergency
measure were also bringing into being a bureaucratic layer within the party
and state, and the banning of factions played into its hands. As Trotsky put it:

> Not until the Tenth Party Congress, held under conditions of
> blockade and famine, growing peasant unrest, and the first stages of
> NEP—which had unleashed petty-bourgeois tendencies—was con-
> sideration given to the possibility of resorting to such an excep-
> tional measure as the banning of factions. It is possible to regard
> the decision of the Tenth Congress as a grave necessity. But in the
> light of later events, one thing is absolutely clear: the banning of
> factions brought the heroic history of Bolshevism to an end and
> made way for its bureaucratic degeneration. (*Writings, 1935-36*, pp.
> 185-86)

In the fall of 1922, Lenin proposed to Trotsky that they form a bloc in
order to wage a battle against bureaucratism and a growing conservative
trend within the Russian Communist Party. The new bureaucratic layer
had begun to accumulate privileges which drew it away from the revolutionary program of the Party. The leading figures within this layer, particularly Joseph Stalin, constituted what was essentially an undeclared faction
which systematically began to undermine the revolutionary program.
Lenin did not call his bloc with Trotsky a "faction" or consider such activity
prohibited by the Tenth Congress resolution. At the same time, he believed
that it constituted a major and necessary challenge to the policies of the
majority of the party's central leadership. He outlined his preliminary ideas
and program of reform in a series of notes and articles. (See Lenin and
Trotsky, *Lenin's Fight Against Stalinism*.)

Unfortunately, a stroke in April 1923, and death in January 1924, prevented Lenin from carrying out the campaign. Thus it fell to Trotsky alone
to launch the struggle to defend the Bolshevik-Leninist program and organizational norms in the Russian Communist Party and the Communist International.

By the fall of 1923 the economic crisis inside the Soviet Union reached
a new level—with widespread unemployment and a massive strike wave in

which some party members participated. The Central Committee of the Russian Communist Party met and discussed further curtailment of credits to the nationalized industries and repressive measures against party members involved in the strikes. In response, Trotsky focused on measures that would address the underlying cause of discontent in the country, and in the party ranks. In October 1923 Trotsky wrote two letters to the Central Committee. In his first letter he outlined the two reasons for

> the marked deterioration of the situation inside the party: (a) the fundamentally improper and unhealthy regime within the party; and (b) the dissatisfaction of the workers and peasants with the grave economic situation that has come about not only as a result of objective difficulties but also because of obvious radical mistakes in economic policy. (*Challenge, 1923-25*, p. 52)

After attempting to resolve the problem within the Central Committee for more than a year, Trotsky concluded that he must take the struggle beyond the Central Committee:

> This raises the danger that the party may be caught unawares by a crisis of exceptional severity; and in that case any comrade who saw the danger but failed to openly call it by name could be rightly accused by the party of placing form above content.
>
> In view of the situation that has developed, I think it is not only my right but my duty to make the true state of affairs known to every party member whom I consider to be sufficiently prepared, mature, self-restrained, and consequently capable of helping the party find a way out of this impasse without factional convulsions and upheavals. (*Challenge, 1923-25*, p. 58)

Soon afterward, 46 prominent Bolsheviks sent a communication to the Central Committee, warning that "the party is to a considerable extent ceasing to be that living independent collectivity which sensitively seizes living reality because it is bound to this reality with a thousand threads." They demanded that "the factional regime must be abolished, and this must be done in the first instance by those who have created it; it must be replaced by a regime of comradely unity and internal party democracy." (*Challenge, 1923-25*, pp. 399, 400)

The majority of the Central Committee, led by a triumvirate composed of Stalin, Zinoviev, and Kamenev, threatened disciplinary action. But, under pressure from the deepening economic crisis, and a growing discontent within the party, the Central Committee opened a literary discussion in the pages of *Pravda*. By December, the supporters of the majority in the Central Committee passed a resolution through which *they* could pose before the masses as being the ones leading the struggle against bureaucratic methods. Although Trotsky saw their action as a maneuver, he signed the resolution and utilized the document in the campaign for party democracy. The "New Course" resolution restated the necessity of the party to collectively discuss the most important problems facing it, and with this document oppositional forces sympathetic to Trotsky's views conducted the campaign for inner-party democracy at party meetings.

This was the beginning of the prolonged struggle of the Left Opposition against the bureaucratic degeneration of the party, the state and the revolution. At various points, many of the leading Bolsheviks joined the protracted struggle of the Opposition, although many ultimately capitulated because of the intense pressure which the bureaucracy was able to exert.

Trotsky himself felt the need to make retreats and compromises. In 1923, while refraining from challenging the Tenth Congress ban, he asserted: "To have the party as a whole participate in the working out and adoption of the resolutions, is to promote temporary ideological groupings that risk transformations into durable groupings and even into factions." In the following year, however, he felt pressured to say that "I have never recognized freedom for groupings inside the party, nor do I now recognize it...." (*Challenge, 1923-25*, pp. 80, 154) By 1925, he was forced, in a letter dictated by the Political Bureau, to disavow the existence of Lenin's Testament and Max Eastman's publication of it. (*Challenge, 1923-25*, pp. 309-15)

In 1923, Trotsky asserted: "As to the theory of the 'permanent revolution,' I see no reason to renounce what I wrote on this subject in 1904, 1905, 1906, and later." (*Challenge, 1923-25*, p. 101) Yet by 1926-27 he felt compelled, repeatedly, to renounce his theory. (*Challenge, 1926-27*, pp. 145, 176-77, 193, 386-87) In order to obtain a "breathing spell" in 1926, Trotsky and other leaders of the Opposition signed a statement in which they demobilized the Opposition as a faction, asserting that "freedom of factions and groupings" was "contrary to Leninism." (*Challenge, 1926-27*, pp. 125-29)

In later years, Trotsky was able to recover those theoretical positions which had been compromised—on Lenin's last struggle against the bureaucracy, on permanent revolution, on the true meaning of democratic-centralist norms. Even in 1923-27, however, Trotsky's refusal to compromise over the essentials of the Bolshevik-Leninist program made it impossible for the bureaucracy to assimilate or neutralize him. Those

Oppositionists who shared this commitment to the revolutionary program of Bolshevism were, consequently, expelled as "Trotskyists."

The challenge of the Left Opposition brings into bold relief a wide range of organizational problems that are of special relevance to a revolutionary party which has taken power. Some of these problems are of a very different character from those faced by a party *before* the revolution. Yet even for a party in its earlier stages, Trotsky's writings in this period provide invaluable insights into the basic organizational principles of a revolutionary party.

1. Function of democracy in democratic centralism

Trotsky saw democracy and centralism as the "two faces of party organization. The question is to harmonize them in the most correct manner, that is, the manner best corresponding to the situation." In a letter published in *Pravda* in December 1923, Trotsky noted "during the last period there was no such equilibrium. The center of gravity wrongly lodged in the apparatus. The initiative of the party was reduced to the minimum." (*Challenge, 1923-25*, p. 124)

This reduces the fighting capacity of the party—disarming it. Yet the "incomparable advantage" of the party lies precisely in being able to draw conclusions on the basis of "a vibrant and active democracy inside the party." Without this "multiple collective experience," the leadership of the party narrows, giving way "to administration by its executive organs (committee, bureau, secretary, etc.). As this regime becomes consolidated, all affairs are concentrated in the hands of a small group, sometimes only of a secretary, who appoints, removes, gives instructions, inflicts penalties, etc." (*Challenge, 1923-25*, p. 77)

a) The responsibility of the ranks

For Trotsky, democracy within the party was a proletarian weapon in the arsenal of the class struggle.

> Leninism cannot be conceived of without theoretical breadth, without a critical analysis of the material bases of the political process. The weapon of Marxist investigation must be constantly sharpened and applied…. As a system of revolutionary action, Leninism presupposed a revolutionary sense sharpened by reflection and experience, which, in the social realm, is equivalent to the muscular sensation in physical labor. (*Challenge, 1923-25*, pp. 98-99)

Thus, political tasks outlined at a party congress were, at best, an approximation of what needed to be done. Only practical experience could confirm the line, force its modification, or prove that such tasks were inadequate. And the most adequate mechanism for reflecting that variety of experience was through the rich internal life of the party, through its internal party democracy. Singleness of action could only be born out of that collective experience.

> The party is above all an action organization. The entire body of its members should be capable of mobilization for combat at any moment, under the leadership of the Central Committee. Such combat-readiness is inconceivable without the unanimity of the party. But it would be the crudest kind of error to think that unanimity can be created by nothing else but official handbook clichés handed down from above. Unanimity is produced by the party as a whole through the constant renewal and accumulation of collective experience, through a collective effort of thought, on the basis of the party's program, rules, traditions, and past experience. This process is inconceivable without differences, criticism, and the clash of ideas. (*Challenge, 1926-27*, p. 113)

Trotsky explained, "it is in contradictions and differences of opinion that the working out of the party's public opinion inevitably takes place. To localize this process *only* within the apparatus, which is then charged to furnish the party with the fruit of its labors in the form of slogans, orders, etc., is to sterilize the party ideologically and politically." Differences within the party were bound to arise in the future, but, as in the past, these could only be resolved by "the party's collective thinking, checking up on itself each time and thereby maintaining the continuity of development." (*Challenge, 1923-25*, pp. 79-80, 100)

Democracy, in other words, is an essential prerequisite for maximizing the possibility of a correct political program. Clearly, the organizational norm of a rich, internal discussion flowed directly from the centrality of developing and improving the party's political program. Or, in Trotsky's words, "Organizational questions are inseparable from questions of program and tactics." (*Third International After Lenin*, p. 158)

In opposition to the "yes men" that the deadening bureaucratic methods bred, Trotsky described a model Bolshevik:

> A Bolshevik is not merely a disciplined person; he is a person who in each case and on each question forges a firm opinion of his own and defends it courageously and independently, not only against his enemies, but inside his own party. Today, perhaps, he will be in the minority in his organization. He will submit, because it is his party. But this does not always signify that he is in the wrong.

Perhaps he saw or understood before the others did a new task or
the necessity of a turn. He will persistently raise the question a second, a third, a tenth time, if need be. Thereby he will render his
party a service, helping it to meet the new task fully armed or to
carry out the necessary turn without organic upheavals, without
factional convulsions. (*Challenge, 1923-25*, p. 127)

A critical-minded approach by each member is a safety device to help
the party correct an incorrect position, or move decisively onto a new path
when a developing situation dictates. For that reason the party does not need

sycophantic functionaries but men who are strongly tempered
morally, permeated with a feeling of personal responsibility, who
on every important question will make it their duty to work out
conscientiously their personal opinion and will defend it coura-
geously by every means that does not violate rationally (that is, not
bureaucratically) understood discipline and unity of action…. That
is why bureaucratic obsequiousness, spurious docility, and all other
manner of empty well-wishers who know what side their bread is
buttered on, cannot be tolerated. What is needed is criticism,
checking of fact, independence of thought, independence of character, the feeling of responsibility, truth toward oneself and toward
one's work. (*Challenge, 1923-25*, pp. 134-35)

b) How the party builds itself

The Party can only carry out its essential programmatic tasks by "exer-
cising the kind of collective leadership that displays the initiative of the
working class…." (*Challenge, 1923-25*, p. 125) How, then, can the individual members, with their varied experiences, be welded together to form
this effective team?

For Trotsky, the answer lay in the interrelationship of the older generation, with its vast revolutionary experience, and the younger generation,
with its freshness and energy. Each generation had both to teach and to
learn from the other. Through this process the essential team had to be
forged, and the revolutionary party strengthened. In offering a definition
of party democracy as applied to the Russian party's situation, Trotsky
stated, in his speech before the Thirteenth Congress,

On the one hand, party democracy is a regime that assures the theoretical, political, and organizational leadership of the old generation of underground Bolsheviks, rich in experience, because if this
leadership is not assured (and only a child could fail to understand
this) the party will not be able to navigate the ship of state and the
ship of the international workers' movement through difficulties,

narrow channels, rocks, and reefs. But at the same time, party democracy is a regime that while assuring the leading position of the older generation, also assures the younger generation access to the high road of Bolshevism and Leninism—not by formal education (such methods cannot accomplish this), but rather by active, independent, practical participation in the political life of the party and the country. (*Challenge, 1923-25*, pp. 152-53)

In another place, Trotsky wrote, "*It is only by a constant active collaboration with the new generation, within the framework of democracy, that the Old Guard will preserve itself as a revolutionary factor.*" (*Challenge, 1923-25*, p. 125)

The only way a revolutionary party can remain a revolutionary party is through a continuing and renewing process, tempered in the class struggle as well as through the party's evaluation of its perspectives. Trotsky pointed out:

The proletarian revolution marches over great heights and depths. There are dips in the road, tunnels, and steep declivities. And there will be an ample supply of these heights and depths for decades to come. That is why the continual selection of revolutionaries, tempering them not only in the struggle of the masses against the enemy but also in the ideological struggle within the party, testing them in the great events and at abrupt turning points, is of decisive importance for the party. Goethe has said that once you acquire a thing, you must win it again and again in order to possess it in reality. (*Challenge, 1928-29*, pp. 192-93)

It is through democracy that the party welds itself together, tests its political line, and reconquers its revolutionary heritage for the next generation. Trotsky compared this process to the development—once the Civil War was over—of the apprentice Red Army commander.

The future commander enters military school. He has neither revolutionary past nor war experience. He is a neophyte. He does not build up the Red Army as the old generation did: he enters a ready-made organization with an internal regime and definite traditions. Here is a clear analogy with the relationship between the young communists and the Old Guard of the party. That is why the means by which the army's fighting tradition, or the party's revolutionary tradition, is transmitted to the young people is of vast importance. Without a continuous lineage, and consequently without a tradition, there cannot be stable progress. But tradition is not a rigid canon or an official manual; it cannot be learned by heart or accepted as gospel; not everything the old generation says can be believed merely 'on its word of honor.' On the contrary the tradition must, so to speak, be conquered by internal travail; it must be worked out by oneself in a critical manner, and in that way assimilated. Otherwise the whole structure will be built on sand. (*Challenge, 1923-25,* pp. 133-34)

For Marxists, approaching the question of party democracy by simply using principles of parliamentarism as applied to party life is not very useful. Nor is it useful to look at the formal limits imposed by party statutes. These questions, maintained Trotsky, are secondary. They can be examined "in the light of our experience" and "necessary modifications" can be introduced. "But what must be modified before anything else is the spirit that reigns in our organizations. Every unit of the party must return to collective initiative, to the right of free and comradely criticism—without fear and without turning back—and to the right of organizational self-determination." Any attempt to write rules and set norms regarding democratic centralism in party statutes must take as its starting point "safeguarding the party against such phenomena as the possibility of bureaucratization of its apparatus, as well as the attendant danger that the party might become isolated from the masses." (*Challenge, 1923-25,* pp. 126,152)

Of necessity the political tasks and economic questions facing the revolutionary party "will unfailingly engender differences of opinion and temporary groupings of opinion." (*Challenge, 1923-25,* p. 85) But such a process is not to be feared, because it is only through internal democracy that Marxists can verify their perspectives. Trotsky asserted: "Without temporary ideological groupings, the ideological life of the party is unthinkable. Nobody has yet discovered any other procedure. And those who have sought to discover it have only shown that their remedy was tantamount to strangling the ideological life of the party." (*Third International After Lenin,* p. 149)

To bottle up differences that exist, to keep silent, to resort to a stereotyped phrase or quotation from Lenin torn out of context—these are the methods of an unhealthy party. As Trotsky noted, if the party is not to discuss differences and decide on the basis of the information presented, then who will make the decision? Responding to a campaign waged in *Pravda* in 1926 that inner-party discussion is harmful and dangerous, Trotsky remarked:

> What is a discussion? It is the formal consideration by the party of the questions which stand before it on which there are differences. Can the party decide these matters without discussing them? It cannot. And if the party is not to decide these questions, who is to decide them for it? This is essentially what it all comes down to—whether someone can decide disputed questions for the party, in

place of the party, and behind the back of the party. (*Challenge, 1926-27*, p. 120)

c) The responsibility of the leadership

For Trotsky, leadership in the party must reflect the collective experience of the party itself. Leadership is elected to carry out the administrative work of the party. It must understand that it is "nothing but the executive mechanism of the collective will." (*Challenge, 1923-25*, p. 126) The Oppositionists quoted Lenin's remark that "the Bolshevik 'general staff' must 'really be backed by the good and conscious will of an army that follows and at the same time directs its general staff.'" (*Challenge, 1926-27*, p. 352)

Trotsky points to the importance of building a leadership team. Thus the responsibility of the leadership is to help the ranks by setting a tone in which decisions can be collectively made. A healthy leadership will "*heed the voices of the broad party masses and must not consider every criticism a manifestation of factionalism and thereby cause conscientious and disciplined party members to withdraw into closed circles and fall into factionalism.*" (*Challenge, 1923-25*, p. 80) Without a genuinely open leadership, the dynamic processes by which the party is welded together are transformed. In their place is the "fragmentation of the party cadres, the removal from the party leadership of valuable elements representing a significant portion of its accumulated experience, and the systematic narrowing down and ideological impoverishment of the leadership core." (*Challenge, 1926-27*, p. 69)

Any attempt to halt bureaucratic methods

> must aim at replacing the mummified bureaucrats with fresh elements closely linked with the life of the collectivity or capable of assuring such a link. And before anything else, the leading posts must be cleared of those who, at the first word of criticism, of objection, or of protest, brandish the thunderbolts of penalties before the critic. The "new course" must begin by making everyone feel that from now on nobody will terrorize the party. (*Challenge, 1923-25*, pp. 126-27)

2. The bureaucratic mode of functioning

Party democracy maximizes the opportunity of the party to develop a correct programmatic line. The bureaucratic method, on the other hand, kills initiative and breeds cynicism within the ranks. A bureaucratic regime

> is the greatest of all dangers—because it paralyzes the vanguard of the proletariat, the main force for resisting the enemy. If a soldier's hands have been tied, the main danger is not the enemy but the

rope which binds the soldier's hands. The present regime ties down the initiative and independent activity of the party…. It weakens the party in the face of the enemy. (*Challenge, 1926-27*, p. 411)

In this context, the growth of party bureaucracy contributes substantially to the development of an incorrect political line—precisely because the bureaucratic method works to *prevent* the line from being corrected:

> All questions of internal and international policy invariably lead us back to the question of the internal party regime. Assuredly, deviations away from the class line in the questions of the Chinese revolution and the English labor movement, in the questions of the economy of the USSR, of wages, of taxes, etc., constitute in themselves a grave danger. But this danger is increased tenfold because the bureaucratic regime binds the party hand and foot and deprives it of any opportunity to correct the line of the leading party tops in a normal manner. (*Third International After Lenin*, p. 159)

In the early years of Trotsky's struggle against the growing bureaucratization, everyone at least formally admitted that the bureaucracy should be checked. But by 1926, the apparatus was ready to redefine party democracy, transforming it into its opposite. As the contradiction between party resolutions and reality widened, the apparatus attempted to overcome the contradiction "by bringing the program down, drastically, to the level of what has existed in practice." (*Challenge, 1926-27*, p. 65)

A 1926 article in *Pravda* summarized a report given by Uglanov, secretary to the Moscow party organization. *Pravda* stated:

> What is the essence of party democracy? Comrade Uglanov gives a clear and concise answer: It is to present the basic tasks facing the party and the country to the party organization in a correct and timely way so that it can resolve them; to draw the broad mass of party members into the discussion and resolution of these problems; to explain the fundamental problems of socialist construction to the proletariat in a correct and timely way; to check the correctness of our policies against the moods of the working class and its individual detachments; and to rectify our line on the basis of such checking. (*Challenge, 1926-27*, p. 62)

In attempting to give the "essence" of democracy, Uglanov in fact defended the essence of bureaucracy—although Trotsky thought the definition suggested a fairly "enlightened" version of bureaucratic functioning. Trotsky noted that:

> To the speaker it was totally self-evident and a foregone conclusion that tasks are presented to the party by the apparatus and only by the

apparatus, and if it presents them "in a timely and correct way," the timeliness and correctness being decided by the apparatus itself....

The party is portrayed as an inert mass that tends to resist and must be *"drawn into"* the discussion of tasks that are *presented* to it by that very same party apparatus.

Going further, we learn that it is democracy "to explain the fundamental problems of socialist reconstruction to the proletariat in a correct and timely way," i.e., the same questions which the apparatus has presented to the party, and into the discussion of which it has drawn the party. Here the one-sided, bureaucratic relationship between the apparatus and the party is extended to the class.

It is democracy "to check the correctness of our policies against the moods of the working class and its individual detachments." The same apparatus that presents the tasks, that draws the party into the discussion of them, and that explains these tasks to the proletariat—this same apparatus checks its policies against the "moods" of the working class in order "to rectify the line on the basis of such checking." Thus, the line is rectified by the very ones who initiated it—the apparatus....

Of free discussion by the party on *all* questions, there is no mention whatsoever. And finally, in his version, the question of responsible and leading individuals being subject to election is totally excluded from the essence of party democracy. (*Challenge, 1926-27*, pp. 63, 65)

Trotsky pointed out that the Russian Communist Party was becoming a party that lived on two separate floors: "the upper story, where things are decided, and the lower story, where all you do is learn of the decisions." (*Challenge, 1923-25*, p. 69) More and more, the apparatus would confront the party "with an already adopted decision, an irreparable situation, an accomplished fact." (*Third International After Lenin*, p. 153)

As a result of the developing hierarchy within the party, where "the real rights of one member of the party at the top (above all, the secretary) are many times greater than the real rights of a hundred members at the bottom" (*Challenge, 1926-27*, p. 352), collective decision making was replaced by a reinforced bureaucratic rule.

The participation of the party ranks in the actual shaping of the party organization is becoming more and more illusory. Over the past year or year and a half a special *party secretary psychology* has been created, the main feature of which is the conviction that the secretary is capable of deciding any and all questions without being familiar with the substance of the matters involved.... This practice is all the more harmful because it dissipates and kills any feeling of responsibility. (*Challenge, 1923-25*, p. 55)

a) What were the objective reasons for the rise of the bureaucracy?

While leading the struggle of the Left Opposition against the bureaucracy in the Russian Communist Party and the Soviet state, Trotsky repeatedly attempted to define the fundamental sources of bureaucracy. This section will examine Trotsky's conclusions on the growth of the bureaucracy and its need to repress any opposition to it as this fight was taking place. It should be kept in mind, however, that Trotsky subsequently modified these conclusions in the light of later events—as the Soviet bureaucracy consolidated itself. (His later views can be found in *The Revolution Betrayed*.)

Trotsky maintained that it is not an adequate answer to blame the rise of bureaucracy within the Russian Communist Party on the country's low cultural level. "After all," Trotsky noted, the party

> counts among its members the most cultured and energetic of the vanguard of the toiling masses, and above all the industrial proletariat. This vanguard is growing quantitatively and qualitatively. Consequently, as far as the regime within the party is concerned, it ought to be steadily becoming more democratic. But in fact it is growing more bureaucratic. (*Challenge, 1926-27*, pp. 67-68)

Nor can one merely blame the weight of the bureaucratic apparatus on the Civil War and on war communism. Trotsky pointed out that "even during the harshest days of war communism, *the system of appointment within the party* was not practiced on one-tenth the scale" that it was by 1923. He remarked that at the party's Twelfth Congress (1923) the party as a whole understood "that the tight hold that characterized the period of war communism should yield to a livelier and broader party responsibility." Instead, the opposite took place. He remembered: "In the cruelest hours of the civil war we argued in the party organizations, and in the press as well, over such issues as the recruitment of specialists, partisan forces versus a regular army, discipline, etc.; while now there is not a trace of such an open exchange of opinions on questions that are really troubling the party." (*Challenge, 1923-25*, pp. 55, 56)

Rather than these explanations, "the fundamental cause of bureaucratization must be sought in the relations between classes." (*Challenge, 1926-27*, p. 68) On an international level, the failure to extend the 1917 Revolution, especially to Germany, meant that the revolutionary upsurge following

World War I had been contained—at least for the time being—by capitalism. This retardation had a demoralizing effect on the world proletariat—and had immediate consequences for the toiling masses in the Soviet Union. Isolated, technologically backward, the Soviet Union was forced, by historical circumstance, to develop its economy while being encircled by capitalist nations that were intent on destroying its economic and political system.

This meant that the New Economic Policy (NEP) which was, in Trotsky's words, "undoubtedly necessary as a road toward socialism, by partially resurrecting capitalism, has also revived forces hostile to socialism." (*Challenge, 1926-27*, p. 390) NEP was adopted to aid the progress of production in the countryside, setting up "a dynamic equilibrium between industry and agriculture, with the socialist elements gaining increasing predominance over the capitalist elements." (*Challenge, 1926-27*, p. 49) "The tempo of economic development" inside the USSR was extremely important, with "the kulaks [rich peasants], the middlemen, the retailers, the concessionaires" capable of being won over to a counterrevolution. To prevent these forces from uniting against the Soviet state, it was necessary to develop "the rational organization of industry and...its coordination with the peasant market." (*Challenge, 1923-25*, pp. 90, 89)

This necessary task, in turn, put the party into close contact with non-working class forces. While "obliged in the next period to assure its internal equilibrium and its revolutionary line by leaning on cells of a *heterogeneous* social composition," the party opened itself up to being influenced by a petty-bourgeois layer. Thus

> the essential source of bureaucratism resides in the necessity of creating and sustaining a state apparatus that unites the interests of the proletariat and those of the peasantry in perfect economic harmony, from which we are still far removed. The necessity of maintaining a permanent army is likewise another important source of bureaucratism. (*Challenge, 1923-25*, pp. 90, 91-2)

The only course open to the Russian Communist Party was fraught with danger. The economic and cultural policies of the party had to be such that

> the proletarian vanguard, the vehicle of these policies, can carry them out, to an ever increasing extent, through free discussion, with control over the apparatus, and with the right to elect it. It is plainly evident that if industry, that is, the base on which the socialist dictatorship rests, lags behind the development of the economy as a whole; if value accumulated in the economy is not distributed along lines that will assure the further ascendancy of socialist tendencies

over capitalist ones; if the difficulties resulting from this are placed first and foremost on the backs of the working class; if wage increases for the workers are delayed, in the midst of a general advance of the economy; if such exceptional fiscal devices as the vodka monopoly become a growing burden on the workers—under such conditions the party apparatus is less and less able to carry out its policies by means of party democracy. The bureaucratization of the party in this case is an expression of the disrupted social equilibrium, which has been and is being tipped to the disadvantage of the proletariat. (*Challenge, 1926-27*, p. 68)

By 1927 less than one-third of all party members were industrial or transportation workers. Over the previous year and a half, the party lost 100,000 factory workers. The social composition of the party's leadership bodies had deteriorated even more rapidly. Industrial workers represented approximately ten percent of the membership of these bodies, while more than three-quarters of the members worked for government agencies. (*Challenge, 1926-27*, pp. 350-51) This marked the triumph of the apparatus-man.

Trotsky, of course, was not saying that the party could "tear itself away from the social and cultural conditions of the country." He maintained that the bureaucratization of the apparatus stemmed from

deep social causes and that the fundamental source of bureaucratization is the state apparatus, in which we find the disputes between classes mixed together with the areas of agreement between classes, and in which the low level of culture of the broad masses of toilers is reflected (as well as that of the working class itself). And because our party is at the head of the state, the state apparatus is the most direct and immediate source of bureaucratic influences on the party.

The question was how to "realize this leadership without merging into the bureaucratic apparatus of the state. (*Challenge, 1923-25*, pp. 92, 158, 76-7)

The bureaucracy flourished with "the *growth* of class influences alien to the proletariat." (*Third International After Lenin*, p. 158) Because of the apparatus's economic policies of the 1920s, industry lagged behind the economic development of the country as a whole. Despite the numerical growth of the proletariat, its social weight declined. And this, in turn, had a negative influence on agriculture, where the kulaks' rapid growth "diminishes the social weight of the poor peasants and agricultural workers and lowers their confidence in the government and in themselves." (*Challenge, 1926-27*, pp. 76-77) Thus, according to Trotsky, the bureaucracy was strengthening the development of class forces hostile to the proletariat, while furthering the demoralization of the workers and village poor.

Trotsky examined the problem of the demoralization of the working class in his 1926 memorandum, "Theses on Revolution and Counterrevolution." He explained that because revolutions are impossible without the participation of the masses on a broad scale, "the hopes engendered by the revolution are always exaggerated." In fact,

> the conquests gained in the struggle do not correspond, and in the nature of things cannot *directly* correspond, with the expectations of the backward masses awakened in large numbers for the first time in the course of the revolution…. The disillusionment of a considerable section of the oppressed masses in the immediate gains of the revolution and—directly connected with this—the decline of the political energy and activity of the revolutionary class engender a revival of confidence among counterrevolutionary classes—both among those overthrown by the revolution but not shattered completely and among those who aided the revolution at a certain phase, but were thrown back in to the camp of reaction by the further development of the revolution. (*Challenge, 1926-27*, p. 166)

Then, looking at the specific character of the Russian Revolution, Trotsky pointed out:

> The October Revolution, to a greater extent than any other in history, aroused the greatest hopes and passions in the popular masses, above all the proletarian masses. After the immense sufferings of 1917-21, the proletarian masses have considerably improved their lot. They cherish this improvement, hopeful of its further development. But at the same time their experience has shown them the extreme gradualness of this improvement which has only now brought them back to the prewar standard of living. This experience is of incalculable significance to the masses, especially the older generation. They have grown more cautious, more skeptical, less directly responsive to revolutionary slogans, less inclined to place confidence in broad generalizations. These moods, which unfolded after the ordeals of the civil war and after the successes of economic reconstruction and have not yet been undone by the new shifts of class forces—these moods constitute the basic political background of party life….
>
> The younger generation, only now growing up, lacks experience in the class struggle and the necessary revolutionary tempering. It does not explore for itself, as did the previous generation, but falls immediately into an environment of the most powerful party and governmental institutions, party tradition, authority, discipline, etc. For the time being this renders it more difficult for the young generation to play an independent role. (*Challenge, 1926-27*, pp. 170-71)

b) How the bureaucratic apparatus functioned

Rakovsky, a collaborator of Trotsky during this period, pointed out that while Lenin was alive, the party apparatus did not wield one-tenth the power it later possessed. Instead of a conscious party democracy, the bloated and self-appointed apparatus fostered:

> (1) garbled versions of the theories of Leninism adapted for the purpose of entrenching the party bureaucracy; (2) abuse of power, which with respect to Communists and workers under the conditions of dictatorship cannot fail to assume monstrous proportions; (3) fraudulent tampering with the entire party electoral machinery; (4) utilization of methods during discussion periods of which bourgeois-fascist authorities could be proud but never a proletarian party (strong-arm squads, hecklers who disrupt meetings, speakers torn from the platform, etc.); (5) the absence of comradely bonds and conscientiousness in personal relations, etc., etc. (*Challenge, 1928-29*, p. 115)

These were the extreme manifestations of the bureaucratic mode of functioning within the party.

The selection of personnel for assignments was a ready-made tool for reinforcing the bureaucratic method. Decisions on appointments, dismissals, and transfers were made "above all, from the point of view of how much they may support or hinder the maintenance of the regime within the party...." (*Challenge, 1925-27*, p. 54) As a consequence, Trotsky perceived, as early as 1923, that:

> There has been created a very broad layer of party workers, belonging to the apparatus of the state or the party, who have totally renounced the idea of holding their own political opinions or at least of openly expressing such opinions, as if they believe that the secretarial hierarchy is the proper apparatus for forming party opinions and making party decisions. Beneath this layer that refrains from having its own opinions lies the broad layer of party masses before whom every decision stands in the form of a summons or command. *Within this basic stratum of the party there is an extraordinary degree of discontent*, some of which is absolutely legitimate and some of which has been provoked by incidental factors. This discontent is not being alleviated through an open exchange of opinions in party meetings or by mass influence on the party organizations (in the election of party committees, secretaries, etc.), but rather it continues to build up in secret and, in time, leads to internal abscesses. (*Challenge, 1923-25*, p. 56)

The bureaucratic apparatus, living on its second floor, developed "cliquism, bureaucratic smugness, and complete disdain for the mood, thoughts, and needs of the party." It used a system "of apparatus terror" which intimidates and silences the ranks of the party. And so, even when the apparatus launched a drive to expose corruption of state or party officials, it found few stepped forward to testify. (*Challenge, 1923-25*, p. 69; *Challenge, 1926-27*, p. 41)

This "centralized, self-sufficient party apparatus" leads "inevitably to the dictatorship of the apparatus, because a class with a disorganized vanguard (and the lack of free discussion, of control over the apparatus, and of election rights means a disorganized vanguard) cannot help but become a mere object in the hands of the leadership of a centralized apparatus...." (*Challenge, 1925-26*, pp. 71-72) Instead of a vibrant, internal life, "the party masses hear only the speeches of the party authorities, all reading from the same schematic study outline. Ties are weakened and confidence in the leadership declines. At party meetings officiousness reigns and, along with it, the inevitable apathy associated with it." (*Challenge, 1926-27*, p. 76)

Trotsky noted that the composition of the leadership in the revolutionary party is a function of the political line. But

> criticism of the CC [Central Committee] is viewed approximately the same way the monarchists used to view *lése majesté*. Such attitudes have nothing in common with Bolshevism. CC membership is not a hereditary or even a lifetime position. The CC is an authoritative body but it is still a party body. The party can replace the CC. And in order to do that, the party must be able to judge the CC. Criticism of the CC, especially on major questions of principle and especially in a precongress period, is the most legitimate right of every party member. To infringe on that right is to turn the party into a helpless chorus for the apparatus, with no will of its own. (*Challenge, 1926-27*, p. 255)

The bureaucratic apparatus reduces the quality of leadership because it is, by definition, a self-selecting group, unrepresentative of the party. Ingrown, this apparatus represents a significant danger to the party. Drawing on the lessons Lenin outlined in "On Slogans," Trotsky commented that the apparatus may prevent the party from being flexible enough when history itself demands it.

> Hence the danger arises that if the turn is too abrupt or too sudden, and if in the preceding period too many elements of inertia and conservatism have accumulated in the leading organs of the party, then the party will prove itself unable to fulfill its leadership at that

supreme and critical moment for which it has been preparing itself in the course of years or decades. The party is ravaged by a crisis, and the movement passes the party by—and heads toward defeat. (*Challenge, 1923-25*, p. 203)

When the party's equilibrium is distorted and thrown off balance by a bureaucratic mode of functioning, the task of welding together the experience of the Old Guard and the youth are turned into their opposite—the corruption of each generation. Trotsky traced how youth, with its independence of spirit, can nonetheless be negatively transformed.

> Under NEP conditions, the youth, having no experience of the class struggle of former times, can rise to the level of Bolshevism only through the independent exercise of its capacity to think, be critical, and test things out in practice. We were warned many times by Vladimir Ilyich about the need to be especially careful and attentive in dealing with ideological processes among the youth. But bureaucratism does the opposite: it clamps the development of youth in a vise, drives their doubts and questions back within them, cuts off criticism, and sows lack of confidence and discouragement on one side and careerism on the other. (*Challenge, 1926-27*, p. 83)

As for the Old Bolsheviks—of whom there were less than 10,000 at the beginning of Trotsky's struggle—many succumbed to the apparatus's intimidation tactics. For the "cadres upon whom the party could rely in the most difficult times are being driven from the ranks in ever greater numbers; they are being reassigned, exiled, persecuted, and replaced everywhere by incidental figures who have never been tested but who make up for it by displaying the quality of unquestioning obedience." (*Challenge, 1926-27*, p. 82) By 1929 Trotsky noted "*At the present moment, not only in the Russian Communist Party but in all the foreign Communist parties without exception, all the elements that built up the International and led it in the period of the first four congresses have been removed* from leadership and cut off from the party." (*Challenge, 1928-29*, p. 209)

And, as a result, the revolutionary continuity between generations was broken on an international scale.

> Five years of official leadership armed with the colossal authority of tradition and with inexhaustible resources, has mutilated Marxism and dislocated brains. A whole revisionist generation has been created, in whose consciousness a mass of reactionary theoretical trash is combined with bureaucratic adventurism. Many European Oppositionists also passed through this school, and they are far from

being free of it. The whole field must be replowed deeply with the plow of Marxism. (*Challenge, 1928-29*, p. 155)

The bureaucracy is concerned not with maintaining a revolutionary political line but rather with maintaining apparatus control of party life. Thus the reasons given for a particular decision may not, in fact, be the real reasons at all, but a convenient cover. For instance, when Trotsky asked what were the real motives for the proposed changes in the Revolutionary Military Committee, Kuibyshev, a member of the apparatus, in a moment of honesty, confessed that they were forced to resort to such deception because "We consider it necessary to wage a struggle against you but we cannot declare you an enemy...." (*Challenge, 1923-25*, p. 57)

As a grouping with an inconsistent political line, the apparatus appointed people who were good at carrying out orders, and penalized the independent thinkers. The apparatus stifled discussion through methods of psychological intimidation, but, especially after it became firmly entrenched, the regime was quite willing to use gangster tactics. Intimidation, after all, is simply an extension of the apparatus's ruthless determination to maintain power. As early as 1923 a group of seven—Zinoviev, Kamenev, Stalin, Bukharin, Rykov and Tomsky, of the Politburo, and Kuibyshev, who was chairman of the Central Control Commission—met in secret and

> decided in advance, without the knowledge of the party, every question on the agenda of the Politburo and Central Committee, and unilaterally decided a number of questions that were never brought before the Politburo at all. It made party assignments in a factional manner. And its members were bound by internal faction discipline.... In Moscow, Leningrad, Kharkov, and other major centers, secret meetings are held, organized by only part of the top brass of the party apparatus, even though they have control of the entire official apparatus. These secret meetings of a select list of people are purely factional in character. Secret documents are read at them, and anyone not belonging to the faction who simply passes on such documents is expelled from the party. (*Challenge, 1926-27*, pp. 86-7)

In time this secret faction itself was torn apart by political differences as more and more a one-man rule gained dominance.

In a healthy revolutionary party, as new questions arise, these, in turn, give "birth to new groupings and shifts." The danger of a bureaucratic clique is that it seeks to transform itself into a "permanent majority, independently of its political line and of the changing tasks of the real majority of the party." Bound by its own secret discipline, the faction "uses the party machine to prevent the party from determining by democratic means where the real majority and minority are." (*Challenge, 1926-27*, p. 106) By its arrogance, the bureaucracy created a factional attitude within the party. As Trotsky noted, "*Bureaucratism of the apparatus is precisely one of the principal sources of factionalism.* It ruthlessly represses criticism and drives discontent back into the depths of the organization. It tends to put the label of factionalism upon any criticism...." (*Challenge, 1923-25*, p. 127)

The bureaucratic group in power in the Soviet Union in the 1920s specifically violated Leninist organizational norms. A 1920 party conference declared "any acts of repression whatsoever against comrades because they are dissidents on one question or another are inadmissible by decision of the party." (*Challenge, 1926-27*, p. 82) Yet, in direct violation of that norm, the apparatus, in the late 1920s, carried out a purge of oppositionists within the Russian Communist Party and the Comintern—for merely expressing their views at party meetings.

Official institutions of the party—including conferences, congresses and plenums—were frequently confronted with decisions that had already been made. Delegates were then forced to rubber-stamp the decision or— given the factional atmosphere—go over to the Opposition. "Thus, before a decision is made, the party knows nothing about it, no matter how important it may be. And after the decision has been brought down on the party's head as a total surprise, one is forbidden to discuss it on pain of being accused of violating discipline." (*Challenge, 1926-27*, p. 115)

The bureaucratic regime had need to distort the actual record of party proceedings. When, in 1927, the party plenum discussed the problems of the revolution in China, Trotsky's views were not even stenographically recorded. In another case, "even the proceedings of the ECCI plenum, against all previous tradition, have not been published in the party press, and in the excerpt from these discussions issued recently for party members Comrade Trotsky's speech is not printed—under the pretext that he did not correct the stenographic text in time." (*Challenge, 1926-27*, p. 247)

Or the documents for the discussion were never printed. Party units were compelled to vote " 'denunciations' of documents that are totally unknown to them." In fact congresses and conferences were called without a preliminary free discussion (such as was always held under Lenin) of all questions by the whole party. "The demand for such a discussion is treated as a violation of party discipline." (*Challenge, 1926-27*, p.353) Conventions, mandated by party procedure, were postponed.

In launching a vicious campaign against Trotsky, the ruling clique prevented the ranks of the party from knowing what Trotsky's political positions were. They distorted Trotsky's real views, cleverly refuting positions that he did not hold, and slandered him, claiming he underestimated the peasantry, etc. On occasion, the apparatus would adopt, without acknowledgement, a proposal the opposition had first put forth—which disoriented even some of the oppositionists.

Over time, the apparatus was able to systematically abolish inner-party democracy—

> in violation of the whole tradition of the Bolshevik Party, in violation of the direct decisions of a series of party congresses. The genuine election of officials in actual practice is dying out. The organizational principles of Bolshevism are being perverted at every step. The party constitution is being systematically changed, to increase the rights at the top and diminish the rights of the base party units. (*Challenge, 1926-27*, p. 352)

Given the growing level of suppression within the Russian Communist party, the apparatus would, from time to time, attempt to maintain its power in the face of its incorrect political line by adjusting the line through "self-criticism." Trotsky noted that

> a correct course can be achieved only by the methods of party criticism, focusing on the basic shifts in line and defects in the party regime that have appeared in the last five years. We must condemn a false policy in order to pave the way for a correct one. As for the "self-criticism" announced in manifestos and articles, up to now this is nothing but a way of venting rank-and-file discontent by denouncing errors of secondary importance and sacrificing one or two hundred bureaucrats as scapegoats. Criticism of the way the policy is carried out is presented as good, healthy, and "businesslike." Criticism of the leadership is said to be destructive, pernicious, oppositional. If the "self-criticism" does not surpass these limits, the entire left-centrist zigzag will be nothing but a harmful fiasco. (*Challenge, 1928-29*, p. 145)

The apparatus was not even interested in "following the day-to-day development of the labor movement and its internal struggles." Instead, it provided "rigidly official information, which is always adapted to the momentary interests of the leading circles." This, Trotsky explained, was due to "the heavy defeats of the international revolution." (*Challenge, 1928-29*, pp. 182-83) These defeats could not be explained because they would disclose the bankruptcy of the leadership.

Party history, just as organizational norms, was a tool for the apparatus. It, too, had to be rewritten, distorted, and turned into a crude tool to maintain the bureaucracy. Events were distorted and prettified. Present leaders were projected into leading roles in the past—when, as in the case of Stalin, they had actually opposed the Bolshevik policy that led to the October Revolution.

> By tearing quotations out of context, by using a biased and one-sided selection of old polemical statements by Lenin in a rude and disloyal way, by hiding from the party other, far more recent statements of Lenin's, by openly falsifying party history and the events of the past, and even more important, by distorting all the questions at present in dispute, and by flagrantly substituting artificial issues for real ones, the group of Stalin and Bukharin, departing farther and farther from the principles of Lenin, is trying to deceive the party into believing that this is a struggle between Leninism and Trotskyism. The struggle is, in actual fact, between Leninism and Stalinist opportunism. (*Challenge, 1926-27*, p. 387)

Trotsky's letter to the Bureau of Party History (see *The Stalin School of Falsification*) contains around fifty quotations and documents demonstrating the methods through which the regime fabricated and distorted Marxist theory and the history of the Russian Revolution in its factional war against the Opposition.

"Theoretical dishonesty" is one of the traits of bureaucratic functioning.

> Ideological dishonesty in a revolutionary leadership is the same as sloppiness in a surgeon. Both inevitably lead to the infection of the organism. However, the theoretical dishonesty of a leadership is neither an accident nor a personal trait: it flows from the contradiction between the principles of Leninism and the ruling clique's determination to control the apparatus. (*Challenge, 1928-29*, p. 183)

The ruling regime also slandered its opposition outside the ranks of the party as well. For the apparatus, the party press was its faction's press. Trotsky contrasts this method with the perspective of Lenin:

> We are firmly convinced that in fundamental political questions the party has nothing to conceal from the non-party working masses, who constitute the class basis of our party, and that those who are not party members must be kept informed about inner-party affairs by means of an objective outline of the different points of view within the party, as was the case under Lenin.

Additionally, Trotsky noted, "The dying out of inner-party democracy leads to a dying out of workers' democracy in general—in the trade unions, and in all other nonparty mass organizations." (*Challenge, 1926-27*, pp. 482, 353) Staggering between "two class lines" (*Challenge, 1926-27*, p. 443), the political program of the apparatus was a reflection of its own material base. Its leftward policies and its rightward policies were merely "the expression of a changing relative influence of classes" both domestically as well as internationally. (*Challenge, 1926-27*, p. 445) The regime's program lacked the political clarity that had characterized the Russian Communist party in its earliest years. As Trotsky remarked to a collaborator in 1928, "even Bukharin's report was lacking in any unifying idea whatsoever. The whole report was made up of patches, like a beggar's pouch." (*Challenge, 1928-29*, p. 181) Because they could not draw a balance sheet and maintain their authority, the apparatus discarded any serious attempt to evaluate the political tasks it had projected. In analyzing the Stalin-Bukharin draft program for the Comintern in 1928, Trotsky commented:

> I consider the draft program a catastrophe in spite of the fact that there are not terrible remarks about our heresy in it. But there are none because, after all the zigzags that have been performed, it is difficult to say in precise programmatic form exactly what that heresy consists of. I tried to do this for the authors of the draft and had to put my pen down helplessly. It is all the more difficult to do this because three-quarters of the draft is spent on trying to imitate this heresy, but the contraband quality of the attempt is still there. The program studiously pretends to be a program of international revolution. In reality it is a program for the construction of socialism in one country, i.e., a program of social patriotism, not of Marxism. The disguise of left phrases changes nothing. The chapter on strategy draws none of the lessons flowing from the experience of the last decade. This signifies the sanctioning of the disastrous policies of the past five years. The section on the East sketches out the perspective for China of a worker-peasant democratic dictatorship which will grow over into a proletarian dictatorship at a later stage. This is preparation for a new Kuomintangism. We must carry out an open ideological struggle against those who did not understand this last fall. In such questions delays and deals are criminal. (*Challenge, 1928-29*, p. 130)

3. Inner-party groups and party norms

The bureaucratic mode of functioning is an attempt to capture, maintain and hold onto the institutions of the party, using them for the faction's own purposes. It denies "the party the chance to use the normal means, provided by the party rules, to make changes in the personnel and policies of the party apparatus." (*Challenge, 1926-27*, p. 87) Thus the normal course of inner-party life is disrupted. Organizational forms which assure every member of the party "an active role in the life of the party, in discussing all problems that come before it, in resolving these problems, and likewise an active role in building the party" are disregarded. (See the Tenth Congress resolution, quoted in *Challenge, 1926-27*, p. 75)

The Tenth Congress (1921) outlined those forms of workers' democracy which "rule out any systematic practices of appointment from above and are best expressed in the broadly based election of all institutions from the bottom up, accountability, control, etc." (*Ibid.*) Trotsky emphasized the importance of a party leadership imbued with the *spirit* of these organizational principles. Mere forms of control, after all, did not prevent Stalin from developing his bureaucratic apparatus. In fact, he *used* Lenin's concept of a rank-and-file control commission to guard against bureaucratism and turned it into yet another instrument of apparatus terror.

The Opposition, led by Trotsky, simply wanted to explain its views to the party. Those in the apparatus—including the editors of *Pravda*—opposed a discussion in the party. To this, Trotsky responded:

> Is it true that discussion is dangerous? That depends on the kind of discussion. Is it dangerous for a workers' cell to talk over the question of why wages have fallen in the midst of a general upturn in the economy? Is it dangerous for a workers' cell to listen to the opinion of the Central Committee majority on this, and the opinion of the Opposition? No, in this there is no danger. All that is needed is for the differing opinions to be presented in strict accordance with party procedure, to be discussed in the proper tone, to be dealt with from all angles, and for the entire party to be provided with the differing opinions to be presented in strict accordance with party procedure, to be discussed in the proper tone, to be dealt with from all angles, and for the entire party to be provided with the necessary documents, so that no one is left in the dark. It is quite a different matter when you have an unceasing, furious, one-sided discussion being conducted in the press and at party meetings—a discussion that degenerates more and more into plain baiting and vilification of the Opposition, while the basic documents in which the Opposition has set forth its point of view are kept hidden from the party. That is the kind of discussion that is dangerous. It poisons the collective mind of the party. It saps the unity of the party. (*Challenge, 1926-27*, p. 123)

Trotsky pointed out that the first congresses of the Comintern "were immeasurably more independent with respect to the Leninist leadership" than subsequent congresses were of their leadership. He recalled that during the Third Congress "Lenin, greatly alarmed, discussed with me (in a 'factional' manner) the question of what tactics we would hold to in case we were to find ourselves in the minority at the congress on the basic strategic questions of the moment. And this danger did threaten us." (*Challenge, 1928-29*, pp. 253-54)

Under Lenin's leadership it was considered "quite normal and to be expected" that a minority in the Bolshevik party and in the Comintern would have access to the ranks. But then a grouping that came together around a particular political question was not frozen into permanence. Party unity is an important goal. Often party unity can be best maintained by a leadership that has the capacity to intelligently resolve differences of opinion within the party. Trotsky outlined three major political disagreements within the Russian Communist party during Lenin's time, and pointed to the various factors that led to the party's resolution of these differences. The Bolshevik seizure of power itself, in October 1917, was hotly debated within the party. In fact, opponents of the uprising published their differences in the non-party press. On this occasion, the danger of a split within the party, or the danger of not taking power in October, was resolved through the successful insurrection. The minority, after the fact, adopted the program of the October Revolution.

In a second case, Trotsky discussed the debate over the Brest-Litovsk treaty. "The partisans of revolutionary war then constituted a genuine faction, with its own central organ, etc." But instead of issuing a ban against the Left Communist faction, the party leadership "adopted more complex methods: it preferred to discuss, to explain, to prove by experience, and to resign itself temporarily to the anomalous phenomenon represented by the existence of an organized faction in its midst. (*Challenge, 1923-25*, pp. 18, 81-82)

In a third case, Trotsky recalled the debate over the trade unions. Here, he noted, the discussion was really an expression of "a profound uneasiness in the party, caused by the excessive prolonging of the economic regime of war communism. The entire economic organism of the country was in a vise. The discussion on the role of the trade unions and of workers' democracy covered up the search for a new economic road." (*Challenge, 1923-25*, p. 82) In fact, the establishing of the New Economic Policy forced the resolution on trade unions to be modified radically within a few months of the congress.

Political disagreements within the party are not always handled in exactly the same fashion. It is the responsibility of the leadership to pay "timely attention to the needs of the moment, which are reflected in the party; and flexibility of the apparatus, which ought not paralyze but rather organize the initiative of the party, and which ought not fear criticism or intimidate the party with the bugbear of factions (intimidation is most often a product of fright)." (*Challenge, 1923-25*, p. 83)

Under Lenin's leadership,

> discussions were held on the basis of the publication and full examination of all the documents concerning the questions in dispute. Without such a system the Communist International cannot become what it must be. The international proletariat still has ahead of it the struggle for power against the very powerful bourgeoisie. This struggle presupposes that the Communist parties will have strong leadership, enjoying moral authority and capable of acting on its own. Such a leadership can be created only over a period of years, by selecting the staunchest, most self-reliant, most consistent, and most courageous representatives of the proletarian vanguard. Not even the most conscientious functionaries can replace revolutionary leaders. The victory of the proletarian revolution in Europe and in the whole world depends, in large measure, on the solution of the problem of revolutionary leadership. The internal regime of the Communist International at present prevents the selection and training of such a leadership. (*Challenge, 1928-29*, p. 31)

But with the replacement of functionaries for a revolutionary leadership, what was once normal procedure fell into disuse, or was transformed into its opposite. Trotsky remarked:

> The criticism of decisions already made is declared a crime. Under a normal party regime that would be correct. Criticism is much more timely during a discussion in preparation for a decision. But the whole crux of the present regime is to drop ready-made decisions on the party's head, decisions that have been discussed and arrived at in gatherings of the ruling faction which are kept secret from the party and at which the disposition of forces is decided in advance, the formal majority is assured in advance, etc. (*Challenge, 1926-27*, pp. 114-15)

The Opposition was forced to break the formal rules of "normal" democratic centralism because of the factional activity of the ruling clique. In the first act after their expulsion from the party, the Oppositionists appealed the decision to the Comintern, admitting: "We Oppositionists have broken the norms of party life. Why? Because we have been deprived of the opportunity to exercise our normal rights as party members." Denied the right to have their documents printed, the Opposition printed and distributed the documents themselves. The real crime was not their distribution of "secret" documents, but that "articles and speeches which should be the property of the entire party have been decreed—yes, even two months before the congress—to be secret documents." (*Challenge, 1928-29*, p. 31; *Challenge 1926-27*, p. 403)

At open party meetings during the precongress discussion, Oppositionists were shouted down or physically abused. They then resorted to holding private meetings, which were attended by thousands of party members, including people who supported the majority line. The Central Committee actually announced that further meetings by party members in private apartments would

> be broken up by force. The very fact that the Central Committee had to resort to such measures, in which one section of the party assumes police duties in relation to another, testifies to the very deepgoing deformations in the party regime. By this the apparatus has declared that it cannot tolerate any propagation of the views of the Opposition, even in the precongress discussion period.... (*Challenge, 1926-27*, p. 475)

On the tenth anniversary of the October Revolution, the Oppositionists organized their own participation in the celebration with a number of posters that counterposed the "truth about the Opposition to the systematic lies and slanders with which both party members and nonparty people are being poisoned." The slogans were "Let us turn our fire against the right: against the kulaks, NEPmen, and bureaucrats." "Carry out Lenin's Last Testament." "For real democracy in the party." (*Challenge, 1926-27*, p. 475; *Challenge, 1928-29*, p. 31) The Opposition noted that this was "abnormal. But this abnormality was imposed upon us by the immeasurably more serious, dangerous, and unhealthy abnormalities of party life and the party regime." (*Challenge, 1926-27*, p. 475)

In their Platform of the Opposition, they declared:

> Let the party find out our real opinions. Let the party familiarize itself with the original documents on the disputed issues, especially on that question of such great international importance, the Chinese revolution. Lenin taught us that when there are differences, we should not believe anything on somebody's say-so, but should demand documents, listen to both of the contending sides, and find out conscientiously what the real disagreements are, setting false issues aside. We, the Opposition, repeat this advice of Lenin's.... We

must create the conditions for an honest debate and an honest resolution of the real issues in dispute, as was always done in Lenin's
time. (*Challenge, 1925-27*, p. 388)

The Opposition did not deny their formal violation of party norms,
but put their technical violation within the context of the crime being done
to the party. The repressive apparatus had destroyed the rules, and the Opposition was simply driven into using whatever tactics it could to reach the
ranks of the party. Its justification was that such extreme methods were the
only way they had to alert the ranks to the dangers facing the revolutionary
party—as the bureaucracy was destroying the party's political program.

4. The program to restore party democracy

The Oppositionists raised a series of demands in the course of their
fight for party democracy. These demands were primarily aimed at encour-
aging the rank-and-file communist to take action—regardless of the repressive apparatus—and put the party and its institutions back on the
correct course. For this only an

> open, clear, and distinct presentation of the basic questions can
> make clear to rank-and-file worker-members of the party why the
> dispute is so sharp, and only this can justify the dispute in their eyes.
> A purely formal presentation of questions of the "inner-party
> regime," "discipline," etc., without any connection to the revolution-
> ary line, is fundamentally contradictory to Bolshevism. The appara-
> tus, which violates the party rules at every turn, at the same time
> strives to place all questions on the plane of formal discipline, or,
> more precisely, of respect for rank. The less the mass of the party
> understands the meaning and depth of the differences, the more the
> apparatus will succeed in this effort. (*Challenge, 1926-27*, p. 453)

Additionally, the Opposition appealed to the elements of the bureaucracy
who thought they were best serving the interests of the revolution by maintaining their silence before this erosion of rights within the party, or who,
at best, were willing to fight for a correct political line only within the secret
meetings of the apparatus.

Trotsky and his co-thinkers had a definite perspective for restoring
party democracy. They called for the following:

1. Respect the right of the party to discuss, and study the essence of
the inner-party differences. This included the publication of documents as well as the right of the party to discuss "in a businesslike
and strictly comradely manner, without personalities and exagger-
ations." (*Challenge, 1926-27*, p. 358)

2. Oppose any violation of party democracy. In order for a discussion to take place, "it is necessary to ensure the most minimal rights for all participants in the discussion. Thugs who throw books and glasses, who whistle and create an uproar and in general deprive party members of the chance to exchange views on the fundamental questions of the revolution, must be called to order." (*Challenge, 1926-27*, p. 451)

3. Confirm and carry out the resolutions on inner-party democracy adopted by the Tenth Party Congress. Those "changes for the worse that have been introduced into the party rules since the Fourteenth Congress (articles, 25, 33, 37, 42, 50, etc.) must be annulled." (*Challenge, 1926-27*, p. 360)

4. Publish—immediately—all of Lenin's articles, speeches, and letters "which have been hidden from the party (I have counted seven groups of documents of that kind)." (*Challenge, 1928-29*, p. 153)

5. Improve the social composition of the party and its leading bodies. "We must carry out the decision of the Thirteenth Congress, in practice annulled by the Fourteenth Congress (against the will of the Opposition)—to the effect that no less than 50 percent of the district committees, the regional committees, etc., should be workers from the factories." (*Challenge, 1926-27*, p. 359)

6. Proletarianize the party apparatus as a whole.

   The apparatus should by no means consist entirely of paid personnel, and it should be regularly replenished with working class members.... One measure for regularly revivifying the party apparatus should be the systematic sending down of a party of the comrades from the apparatus into industry and other rank-and-file work. We must struggle against the tendency of secretaries to make themselves irremovable. We must establish definite terms for the occupation of secretarial and other responsible posts. (*Challenge, 1926-27*, p. 360)

7. Reduce—to about twenty percent—the party's budget (as well as its paid apparatus). "The party budget is the main instrument of the terrible corruption of the apparatus and the basis of its omnipotence. We need an open budget, fully under party control." (*Challenge, 1927-28*, p. 153)

8. Reinstate the expelled Oppositionists to party membership.

9. Reconstruct the Central Control Commission "in the real spirit of Lenin's advice. Members of the Central Control Commission must be: (a) closely associated with the masses; (b) independent of the apparatus; (c) possessed of authority in the party." Only in this way,

the Opposition noted, "can real confidence in the Central Control Commission be restored and its authority raised to the necessary level." (*Challenge, 1926-27*, p. 361)

10. Reorganize party education "along the line of study of the works of Marx, Engels, and Lenin, driving out of circulation the false interpretations of Marxism and Leninism now being manufactured on a large scale." (*Challenge, 1926-27*, p. 361)

11. Work to insure greater equality within the party and among the masses of workers.

> As early as the Twelfth Congress the party noticed the danger, under NEP, of a degeneration of that part of the party workers whose activities bring them into contact with the bourgeoisie. It is necessary to: 'Work out completely adequate practical measures to eliminate inequality (in living conditions, wages, etc.) between the specialists and functionaries, on the one hand, and the masses of workers, on the other, insofar as this inequality destroys democracy and is a source of corruption of the party and lowering of the authority of Communists.' (*Challenge, 1926-27*, p. 360)

12. Elect a leadership—through a secret ballot, as a means of reducing the pressures of the apparatus—that can carry out this program.

Trotsky summarized the tasks this way:

> *To carry out a left, proletarian course, a Leninist course, our party must have a new orientation, from top to bottom, and a realignment of forces.* Those are processes that would have to develop in a serious way over a long period. The party must be allowed once again to have its own free, collective thinking, its own powerful and resilient will. The party must stop being afraid of the apparatus. We must achieve conditions such that the apparatus could not and would not dare try to intimidate the party. The party must once again become—the party. (*Challenge, 1928-29*, p. 138)

Unfortunately, the program of the Opposition was not adopted. Instead, thousands of Oppositionists were expelled from the party, arrested, sent to exile colonies and labor camps. (Later, during the Great Terror of the 1930s, most of them were killed.)

Trotsky was banished from the USSR in 1929. From his foreign exile, he continued to fight for Bolshevik-Leninist political and organizational principles.

Toward the World Party of Socialist Revolution

There is a consistency in Trotsky's views on organizational principles, from the time he embraced Bolshevism to the time of his death. At the same time, there is nothing static or schematic about them. They were characterized by an inherent dynamism which reflected the dialectics of revolutionary struggle. "First of all," he wrote,

> it is necessary to define strategic problems and tactical methods correctly in order to solve them. The organizational forms should correspond to the strategy and the tactic. Only a correct policy can guarantee a healthy party regime. This, it is understood, does not mean that the development of the party does not raise organizational problems as such. But it means that the formula for democratic centralism must inevitably find a different expression in the parties of different countries and in different stages of development of one and the same party. (*Writings, 1937-38*, p. 90)

Trotsky went on to explain that "democracy and centralism do not at all find themselves in an invariable ratio to one another. Everything depends on the concrete circumstances, on the political situation in the country, on the strength of the party and its experience, on the general level of its members, on the authority the leadership has succeeded in winning. Before a conference, when the problem is one of formulating a political line for the next period, democracy triumphs over centralism. When the problem is political action, centralism subordinates democracy to itself. Democracy again asserts its rights when the party feels the need to examine critically its own struggle, at moments it is violated and then again reestablished." (*Writings, 1937-38*, p. 90)

Trotsky believed that "it is necessary, of course, to fight against every individual mistake of the leadership, every injustice, and the like." But he also cautioned: "The maturity of each member of the party expresses itself particularly in the fact that he does not demand from the party regime more than it can give…. It is necessary to assess these 'injustices' and 'mistakes' not by themselves but in connection with the general development of the party both on a national and international scale." (*Writings, 1937-38*, p. 90)

Similarly, one of the best ways to grasp Trotsky's views on organizational principles is to examine them in connection with his involvement in the struggle to forge such a party—the World Party of Socialist Revolution (Fourth International). From 1929 to 1933, he was the leader of the International Left Opposition (ILO), which hoped to reform the Communist (or Third) International; but in 1933 the goal became the creation of a new international. The ILO became the International Communist League (ICL). Some of its sections briefly entered Social Democratic parties of the Second (Labor and Socialist) International for the purpose of winning over leftward-moving forces to the revolutionary perspective of the new international. By 1938, the strengthened Trotskyist forces were able to make the Fourth International a reality.

The complexity of these developments was enhanced by the larger social and political realities in which they unfolded: a world-wide collapse of the capitalist economy, the immense class-struggle upsurge of a radicalized working class, the rising tide of fascism, the accelerating degeneration and ferocity of Stalinism, the illusions engendered in the workers' movement by the reformist People's Front, and the steady approach of a second eruption of imperialist slaughter.

From Trotsky's struggles in this context come some of the richest insights into the organizational principles of the revolutionary party.

1. The integrity of the revolutionary program

Trotsky believed that it was impossible to separate the organizational question from the question of the revolutionary program. "The interests of the class cannot be defended otherwise than by creating the party," he wrote in 1932.

> The class, taken by itself, is only material for exploitation. The proletariat assumes an independent role only at that moment when from a social class in itself it becomes a political class for itself. This cannot take place otherwise than through the medium of a party. The

party is that historical organ by means of which the class becomes class conscious. (*The Struggle Against Fascism in Germany*, p. 163)

At the same time, Trotsky did not move from this generalization to an idealized view of the revolutionary party. When he still considered the Communist Party (despite its degeneration since Lenin's death) to be the revolutionary vanguard, he asserted: "The historical interests of the proletariat find their expression in the Communist Party—when its policies are correct." (*The Struggle Against Fascism in Germany*, p. 163) Until the summer of 1933, he considered the function of the International Left Opposition to be reforming the Communist International and Communist parties so that their policies would constitute an effective revolutionary program.

Trotsky believed that "in some situations victory is possible even with a very bad policy." (*Writings, 1930-31*, p. 293) Elaborating on this, he explained:

> The strategy of the party is an exceedingly important element of the proletarian revolution. But it is by no means the only factor. With an exceptionally favorable relation of forces the proletariat can come to power even under a non-Marxist leadership. This was the case for example in the Paris Commune [of 1871] and, in a period which lies closer to us, in Hungary [in 1919]. The depth of the disintegration of the enemy camp, its political demoralization, the worthlessness of its leaders, can assure decisive superiority to the proletariat for a certain time even if its own leadership is weak. (*Writings, 1932-33*, p.35)

No less significant, however, is what Trotsky added:

> But in the first place, there is nothing to guarantee such a 'fortunate' coincidence of circumstances; it represents the exception rather than the rule. Second, the victory obtained under such conditions remains, as the same two examples—Paris and Hungary—prove, exceedingly unstable. To weaken the struggle against Stalinism on the ground that under certain conditions even the Stalinist leadership would prove unable to prevent the victory of the proletariat...would be to stand Marxist politics on its head. (*Writings, 1932-33*, p. 35)

Trotsky insisted that "to adapt ourselves to the prejudices of the Stalinists instead of appealing to the judgment of the Communists" and

> to blur our difference with centrism [Trotsky at this time characterized Stalinist policies as being "centrist," between reformism and revolutionary politics] in the name of facilitating "unity" would mean not only to commit political suicide, but also to cover up,

strengthen and nourish all the negative features of bureaucratic centrism, and by that fact alone help the reactionary currents within it
against the revolutionary tendencies. (*Writings, 1932-33*, p.35)

Trotsky made similar points about relating to centrist currents in the
Social Democracy. A German centrist urged a conciliatory policy toward
the Norwegian Labor Party, the Independent Labor Party of Britain, and
other groups, suggesting that future events could transform them from
being "as they are" to "as they should be." Trotsky was unwise, he argued, to
"anticipate developments" by sharply polemicizing against such groups.
Trotsky responded:

> The accusations many comrades raise against us in this connection
> are nothing but the worst aspects of the old [pre-1917] "Trotskyism."
> More than once, I developed all of these arguments in both written
> and oral form against Lenin three decades ago. At that time, I too
> wished to make a distinction between Menshevism or its left wing
> "as it was" and "as it should be" according to my analysis, and I re-
> garded Lenin's efforts at separation to be harmful. Moreover, Marx
> and Engels throughout their lives were looked upon as "disruptive el-
> ements" by other groups; Lenin too…until the victory, after which
> they began to praise his sense of expediency without having properly
> understood the long and difficult work of selection and education.
> The school of Marx-Engels-Lenin is good enough that we can all
> learn something from it. (*Supplement, 1929-33*, p. 283)

Of course, Trotsky was convinced that practical united fronts with reformist and centrist groups were necessary to defend the immediate interests of the working class as well as to strengthen the development of
revolutionary tendencies within these other groups—and his 1932 polemic
on the Nazi threat in Germany, *What Next?*, was devoted to explaining this.
In this very work, however, he stressed that "it is imperative that nothing be
hushed, that good intentions be not accepted for deeds, and that all things
be called by their names." He added: "Just now, at this very moment, when
events are pressing down on the Communist Party, we must help the
events with the onset of our criticism." (*The Struggle Against Fascism in
Germany*, pp. 165, 205-08)

A 1929 letter to a Czech comrade further illuminates this point. The
comrade had formally distanced himself from the "Trotskyist" label. Trotsky
wrote:

> You consider that so-called "Trotskyism" is in fact an application of
> the methods of Marx and Lenin to the contemporary period. If you
> mark yourself off from Trotskyism it is, as you explain, not from

considerations of principle but from tactical ones. The members of the [Communist] party are so confused, in your words, by the specter of "Trotskyism" that it is necessary for the time being to present our views in disguise, and not declare openly that they are the views of the Communist Left Opposition.

Such a method "contradicts the whole history of Bolshevism," Trotsky asserted, and he went on to explain:

> You cannot subject the contemporary errors to criticism and propose a correct solution without expounding the views officially condemned under the name of "Trotskyism." And if for pedagogical reasons you distance yourself in words from Trotskyism, there still remains politically the question of your relation to a definite international tendency: the Left Opposition. You risk falling victim tomorrow to the contradictions of your position. One of two things: either you must each time make clear in what you disagree with the Left Opposition, and consequently wage a factional struggle against it—or you will be forced to take off your mask and admit that you were only pretending to be an "anti-Trotskyist" in order to defend the ideas of the Communist Left Opposition. I do not know which is worse.
>
> No, a game of hide-and-seek in politics is an absolutely impermissible thing. I have already quoted several times for various reasons the words of a certain French writer: "If you hide your soul from others, in the end you will no longer be able to find it yourself." (*Writings, 1929*, pp. 180-81)

Trotsky applied the same methodology to the internal affairs of the International Left Opposition. In one letter to the French Communist League, he wrote characteristically: "I am giving you my opinion with total frankness and sharpness because I think that revolutionaries have no need for internal diplomacy and because experience shows that chronic crises are not solved by sugary speeches." (*Writings, 1930-31*, p. 329) These "chronic crises" were caused, in Trotsky's opinion, by a deep divergence of principled programmatic perspectives. This is a clear illustration of the primary importance of genuine unity around a program for the cohesion of a revolutionary organization. He wrote:

> Obviously it is extremely desirable to safeguard the unity of the organization. But there *are* situations…in which two groups pull in opposite directions in so obvious a fashion that it paralyzes the life of the organization. What remains to be done? Above all, every possibility of an honest accord must be thoroughly pursued. But if these attempts have no result, there remains only to say to each

other: let us try to work separately and in six months or more, we will see which of us is right, and then perhaps we will meet each other seriously on the common path. Such an action is called a split. But at times a split is a lesser evil. An organization that is smaller but more unanimous can have enormous success with a correct policy, while an organization which is torn by internal strife is condemned to rot. (*Writings, 1930-31*, p. 328)

An unwavering commitment to the integrity of the revolutionary program remained a characteristic of the Trotskyist movement. It is written into the founding document of the Fourth International:

The Fourth International...takes it stand completely on Marxism as the only revolutionary doctrine that enables one to understand reality, unearth the cause behind the defeats [of the workers' movement] and consciously prepare for victory. The Fourth International continues the tradition of Bolshevism which first showed the proletariat how to conquer power.... If our International be still weak in numbers, it is strong in doctrine, program, tradition, in the incomparable tempering of its cadres. Who does not perceive this today, let him in the meantime stand aside. Tomorrow it will become more evident. (*The Transitional Program for Socialist Revolution*, pp. 107, 111)

2. Functions of party democracy

In a list of the "fundamental principles of the International Left Opposition" written in 1933, Trotsky included the following: "Recognition of *party democracy* not only in words but also in fact; ruthless condemnation of the Stalinist plebiscitary regime (the rule of usurpers, gagging the thought and will of the party, deliberate suppression of information from the party, etc.)." (*Writings, 1932-33*, p. 53) This was basic to the ILO from the very beginning. Writing in 1930, for example, Trotsky argued:

In principle,...I think we should proceed as democratically as possible. What we have in the ranks of the Opposition are cadres; they must be trained, trained to the point of complete self-reliance. That will not come about by their believing in a mighty International Secretariat, but rather through their taking part on all questions in all actions which will gradually lead to the creation of a capable center. (*Supplement, 1929-33*, p. 46)

In the same year, Trotsky had elaborated as follows:

The Opposition needs a democratic internal regime. The cadres can only be educated if all questions are debated by the *whole* Opposition, without fear of 'lack of preparation,' insufficiency on the plane of theory, etc. Revolutionaries grow as their tasks become greater. Questions of revolutionary tactics and internal questions facing the opposition should be the property of *every* member of the Opposition organization. Experience testifies clearly enough that decisions made in the corridors and deliberations in closed circles yield nothing, lead to nothing. Only keeping the ranks of the Opposition informed on all questions, including those in dispute, will immediately change the situation, introduce clarity, force each comrade to follow his line of thinking to its conclusion, and thereby push things forward. (*Writings, 1930*, p. 297)

In 1932, Trotsky offered an illuminating contrast between a party operating according to Bolshevik norms and the Communist parties that had come under the sway of Stalinist norms. "The strength of a revolutionary party," he wrote,

consists in the independence of its vanguard, which checks and selects its cadres and, while educating its leaders, gradually elevates them by its confidence. This creates an unbroken connection between the cadres and the mass, between the leaders and the cadres, and it induces in the entire leadership an inward confidence in themselves. There is nothing of the kind in the contemporary Communist parties! The leaders are appointed. They handpick their aides. The rank and file of the masses is forced to accept the appointed leaders, around whom there is built up the artificial atmosphere of publicity. The cadres depend upon the upper crust and not upon the underlying masses.

The result of this bureaucratic-centralism, Trotsky noted, was a veering away from the revolutionary program: "Thus, throughout the entire Comintern a closed bureaucratic stratum is being created which constitutes a culture broth for the bacilli of centrism. (*The Struggle Against Fascism in Germany*, pp. 216, 217)Centrism, of course, should not be confused with *centralism*. According to Trotsky, "Centrism is composed of all those trends within the proletariat and on its periphery which are distributed between reformism and Marxism, and which most often represent various stages of evolution from reformism to Marxism—and vice versa." (*The Struggle Against Fascism in Germany*, pp. 210-11)

As we noted earlier, Trotsky counterposed to this bureaucratic-centrist "culture broth" a revolutionary political culture which flowed from the dialectical interpenetration of a revolutionary program, internal democracy and organizational centralism. "We Bolshevik-Leninists need democracy for the proletarian vanguard," Trotsky had written in 1929, "as a weapon in the struggle with opportunism and for the preparation of revolution."

(*Writings, 1929*, p. 183) In the following year, he emphasized: "For my part, I believe that every member of the organization can and must know, analyze, and criticize all the questions that form the content of our activity. There are no 'limits' for anyone. That is the ABC of party democracy." (*Writings, 1930*, p. 301)

Internal democracy was indispensable for collectively evaluating and absorbing the common experience that was the basis for the necessary political culture, or the internal 'public opinion,' of the party. As Trotsky commented, "the [organization's] program holds water only in the event that its text is tied up with the revolutionary experience of the party and with the lessons gained from battles which have entered the flesh and blood of its cadres." (*The Struggle Against Fascism in Germany*, pp. 199-200) This living program and political culture, in turn, were necessary for internal democracy: "Really healthy party democracy presupposes a certain public opinion [in our organization], which has crystallized itself out of common experience." (*Supplement, 1929-33*, p. 141) The connection of these themes to the requirements of revolutionary centralism was explained by Trotsky in this way:

> The foundation of party democracy is timely and complete *information*, available to all members of the organization and covering all the important questions of their life and struggle. Discipline can be built up only on a conscious assimilation of the policies of the organization by all its members and on confidence in its leadership. Such confidence can be won only gradually, in the course of common struggle and reciprocal influence. The iron discipline which is needed cannot be achieved by naked command. The revolutionary organization cannot do without the punishment of undisciplined and disruptive elements; but such disciplinary measures can be applied only as a last resort and, moreover, on the condition of solid support from the public opinion of the majority of the organization.
>
> The frequent practical objections, based on the "loss of time" in abiding by democratic methods, amount to short-sighted opportunism. The education and consolidation of the organization is a most important task. Neither time nor effort should be spared for its fulfillment. Moreover, party democracy, as the only conceivable guarantee against unprincipled conflicts and unmotivated splits, in the last analysis does not increase the overhead costs of development but reduces them. Only through the constant and conscientious adherence to the methods of democracy can the leadership undertake important steps on its own responsibility in truly emergency cases without provoking disorganization or dissatisfaction. (*Writings, 1932-33*, pp. 57-8)

Trotsky gave considerable attention to the question of how to handle differences in the revolutionary organization. One key was whether such differences had a political basis. In regard to dissensions arising within the Communist League of America in the early 1930s, he advised: "Given the absence or at least the nonobviousness of the principled [political] basis of the struggle between the groups, *conciliationism is quite justified and progressive* in the League's internal life." In the same period, differences arose in the German section which—representing a political divergence—required different measures:

> Naturally in the presence of serious and lasting differences of opinion an open discussion is inevitable and indispensable. Although it weakens the organization temporarily, it is immeasurably more fruitful than an organizational struggle behind the scenes or half-concealed "allusions" in the press, which bring no results to anybody and only poison the atmosphere. (*Writings, 1932-33*, pp. 127, 32)

The insistence on the strict subordination of nonpolitical differences to principled politics and the insistence on taking political differences with the utmost seriousness were characteristic of Trotsky. In a criticism of the Spanish section in 1932, he wrote:

> It is true that I myself met some comrades in the ranks of the Left Opposition who speak of the internal ideological struggles in a belittling sense, calling them "quibbles, intrigues." Such comrades have not learned in the school of Marx and Lenin. In order to prepare ourselves for the great struggles, we must learn to be steadfast and uncompromising in all the current principled questions, even when they are of a minor character. It is most frequently the case that those comrades who call the principled struggles "intrigues" are precisely the ones who display the ability for real intrigues when someone steps on their corns. A lack of concern about principled questions characterize many of those who landed by accident in the ranks of the Left Opposition. (*The Spanish Revolution*, pp. 176-77)

The manner in which differences are discussed, both within the vanguard organization and within the workers' movement, was a matter of special concern for Trotsky. He was particularly repelled by the factional stridency and sometimes violent sectarianism of "third period" Stalinism. "Within the ranks of Communism and the entire proletariat there must be free discussion," he wrote, "without breaking up meetings, without falsified citations, without venomous vilification—but an honest interchange of opinions on the basis of proletarian democracy. It was thus that we conducted debates with all parties and within our own party throughout the entire year of 1917." (*The Struggle Against Fascism in Germany*, pp. 253-54)

The leadership of the revolutionary organization bears special responsibility in such matters, according to Trotsky. In a letter to the leadership of the German section in 1930, Trotsky warned:

> If the leadership wants to gain authority (and it is duty-bound to want this) it must not proceed as if it already possesses unshatterable authority and must at first base itself as little as possible on its purely formal rights. The Executive must retain a quiet, friendly tone and show its utmost patience, especially towards its opponents. The Executive cannot gain any authority if it does not show in actuality to the entire organization its complete objectivity and conscientiousness in all sorts of conflicts and its concern about the organization as such. Only on this kind of authority, which cannot be achieved in one day, can organizational steps, disciplinary measures, etc., be based. Without this, the organization cannot live. The attempt to use disciplinary measures without the necessary authority and without the conviction of the organization as to the correctness of these measures leads inevitably not to a strengthening of the organization but to its weakening, and above all to the collapse of the Executive itself. (*Writings, 1930-31*, p. 143)

Writing about the same problem one year later, Trotsky added that

> while retaining firmness on the political line, [the leadership should] exercise the greatest caution and mildness, the greatest possible tolerance and tactfulness in all personal conflicts and misunderstandings.... In the time that has passed since the communication quoted above, the Executive has unfortunately increased administrative measures enormously without increasing its authority in the least. (*Writings, 1930-31*, p. 143)

As we have already seen, Trotsky did not believe that a healthy party democracy was possible in the absence of "revolutionary experience" and "lessons gained in battles" of the class struggle. Nothing is so alien to Trotskyism as abstentionism in the face of actual, ongoing mass struggles. As he explained in a 1932 communication to the Spanish section:

> A political group that stayed outside of the actual movement and occupied itself with criticisms after the events, especially under revolutionary conditions, would be rejected by the working class. I do not doubt for a moment that the majority of the Bolshevik-Leninists in the regions have participated in all the mass movements, even when they regarded them as not conforming to their own purposes. A revolutionist criticizes not from the outside but

from the very heart of the movement itself. (*The Spanish Revolution*, p. 172)

Writing in the following year about problems in the Communist League of America, he asserted: "A genuine solution to the internal difficulties can only be found along the path of expanding mass work." (*Writings, 1932-33*, p. 213) Elaborating on this, Trotsky wrote that "serious successes in the field of mass work will inevitably produce a favorable influence upon internal relations and in every case provoke a radical regroupment by gradual isolation of demoralized elements." (*Supplement, 1929-33*, p. 213) Obviously, effective involvement in mass work both contributed to *and required the existence of* healthy party democracy.

The Left Opposition's turn to root itself in the industrial working class, and to draw significant numbers of working-class militants into its ranks, made such organizational norms more necessary than ever: "The sections of the Left Opposition, originating out of small propaganda groups, gradually are being transformed into workers' organizations. This transition puts the tasks of party democracy in first place." (*Writings, 1932-33*, p. 57)

3. Stressing centralism

In 1933, Trotsky gave special stress to the *centralist* imperatives in democratic centralism. It is highly instructive to note the reasons for this. In the wake of the utter failure of the Stalinist-dominated Comintern to resist effectively or evaluate critically the Nazi triumph in Germany, Trotsky and the International Left Opposition drew the conclusion that it would be impossible to reform the Comintern.

> On August 19 the plenum (International Secretariat) [of the ILO] adopted a decision of great political responsibility: the break with the Comintern and the course of [building] a new International. The first result of the new orientation was the principled document of four organizations opening up the era of the preparation for the new International.... In the full meaning of the word, we are entering a new epoch; from propaganda circles we are becoming fighting political organizations of the proletariat. (*Writings, 1933-34*, p. 88)

The possibility of creating a new, mass Leninist international had opened up. The International Left Opposition, the Socialist Workers Party of Germany (SAP), the Independent Socialist Party of Holland (OSP), and the Revolutionary Socialist Party of Holland (RSP) joined together in "The Declaration of the Four, On the Necessity and Principles of a New International." The four organizations had declared: "The undersigned obligate themselves to direct all their forces to the formation of this International in the shortest possible time on the firm foundation of the theoretical and strategic principles laid down by Marx and Lenin." (*Writings, 1933-34*, p. 51)

The ILO had an important network of small groupings throughout the world, but the SAP had a membership of 14,000; the RSP had 950 members and a trade union base of 23,000; the OSP had 7,000 members. The prospects seemed good for even more substantial gains.

Before examining the centralist stress in Trotsky's formulations of this period, it is worth seeing what the ILO had to say about party democracy in its joint statement with the other three groups:

> *Party democracy* is a necessary prerequisite for the healthy development of revolutionary proletarian parties on a national as well as an international scale. Without freedom of criticism, without the election of functionaries from top to bottom, without the control of the apparatus by the rank and file, no truly revolutionary party is possible.
>
> The need of secrecy *under conditions of illegality* changes completely the forms of the internal life of a revolutionary party and makes wide discussions and elections difficult, if not altogether impossible. But even under the most difficult conditions and circumstances, the basic demands of a healthy party regime retain their full force: honest information about the party, freedom of criticism and a real inner unity between the leadership and the party majority. Having suppressed and crushed the will of the revolutionary workers, the reformist bureaucracy turned the Social Democracy and the trade unions into impotent bodies despite their memberships numbering in the millions. Having stifled inner democracy, the Stalinist bureaucracy also stifled the Comintern. The new International, as well as the parties adhering thereto, must build their entire inner life on the basis of democratic centralism. (*Writings, 1933-34*, pp. 51-2)

This had always been, and continued to be, the perspective of the ILO and the Trotskyist movement. But the change in the ILO's perspectives— from functioning as an expelled oppositional faction of the Communist International to striving to build a new international with leftward-moving socialist currents—called for a new emphasis on the democratic centralist norms within the ILO: "In close connection with the new orientation, it is necessary to pose in a new manner the questions of organization, discipline and leadership." (*Writings, 1933-34*, p. 90)

Trotsky felt that there were two problems which arose in the face of the new orientation: the problem of transition from relatively small propaganda circles to growing organizations actively engaged in mass struggles; and the problem of maintaining the integrity of the Bolshevik-Leninist program during a regroupment effort with leftward-moving (but still largely left-centrist) organizations.

In regard to the first problem, he was particularly concerned with difficulties which had cropped up in the French section of the ILO. He argued:

> No matter what the origin of the discontent, conflicts, personal friction, etc., may have been, all the old disagreements must of necessity group themselves now around the basic alternatives: *forward* to a wide arena of the Fourth International or *backward* to small circles stewing in their own juice.
>
> Lifeless, sectarian elements of the French League, as well as of other sections, feel that the ground is slipping from under their feet. The coming out on a wider arena frightens them, as their whole psychology is adapted to an atmosphere of closed circles.
>
> …Since…the Left Opposition formed itself in the struggle with monstrous bureaucratism, many quasi-oppositionists have concluded that inside the Opposition "everything is permitted." In the French League and on its periphery prevail practices that have nothing in common with a revolutionary proletarian organization. Separate groups and individuals easily change their political position or in general are not concerned about it, devoting their time and effort to the discrediting of the Left Opposition, to personal squabbles, insinuations and organizational sabotage. (*Writings, 1933-34*, pp. 89, 90)

Trotsky insisted that "personal squabbles" must be utterly subordinated to "political positions" in a revolutionary organization. He also insisted that nothing should be allowed to block the new outward-reaching orientation and involvement in living struggles in the "wider arena." Otherwise the ILO would degenerate. He went on to observe:

> Any defense measure by the organization against decomposing elements, any appeal to discipline, any repression was described as Stalinism by some members of our own organization. By this they only showed that they are far from understanding Stalinism as well as the spirit of a truly revolutionary organization. The history of Bolshevism has been, from its very first steps, the history of educating an organization in the spirit of iron discipline. The Bolsheviks were originally called the "hard," the Mensheviks the "soft," because the former stood for a harsh, revolutionary discipline while the latter replaced it by mutual indulgence, leniency, vagueness. The organizational methods of Menshevism are inimical to a proletarian organization no less than Stalinist bureaucratism….

Bolshevik-Leninists reject democracy without centralism as an expression of petty-bourgeois content. (*Writings, 1933-34*, pp. 90-1)

Trotsky highlighted the seriousness of his position in these conclusions:

We are making an important revolutionary turn. At such moments inner crises or splits are absolutely inevitable. To fear them is to substitute petty-bourgeois sentimentalism and personal scheming for revolutionary policy.... Under these conditions, a splitting off of a part of the League will be a great step forward.... What will be lost—partly only temporarily—will be regained a hundred fold already at the next stage. The League will finally get the possibility of transforming itself into a fighting organization of the workers. (*Writings, 1933-34*, p. 91)

Related to the problem of transition was the problem of maintaining the integrity of the Bolshevik-Leninist political program in the face of the new situation. In this, he stressed the exceptional importance of the International Secretariat of the ILO:

The work of the International Secretariat has now acquired an absolutely exceptional importance. In addition to the old tasks of uniting the numerous sections and directing their revolutionary work, the Secretariat (plenum) has now become the representative of the entire Left Opposition within the Bloc of Four, which holds aloft the banner of the new International. Beginning right now, the Secretariat must carefully follow the activity of its allies, exchange experiences and criticism with them, participate in elaborating the program of the new International, organize conferences with sympathizing organizations, etc., etc.... The Secretariat can accomplish these historic tasks only if it has real internal cohesion as well as support on all sides from all the sections.

All serious Bolshevik-Leninists reject with indignation unprincipled insinuations addressed to the Secretariat, attacks on its authority, and direct violations of its decisions. Strong leadership centers do not fall from the sky. They are formed through experience in accordance with the development and maturity of the organizations themselves. The elementary condition for the formation of a strong center is a Marxist approach to the principle of centralism, the authority of the leadership, and discipline.

...Any attempt to weaken the IS and undermine its authority must be all the more mercilessly denounced since this is tantamount to disarming the Bolshevik-Leninists, with respect to our allies as well as our enemies. (*Supplement, 1929-33*, pp. 301-02)

It is significant that Trotsky emphasized that—in regard to both the ILO and its individual national sections—"the principle of centralism, the authority of the leadership, and discipline" could only be effective if rooted in internal democracy, and he offered practical suggestions on how the authority of national and international leaderships could be more firmly established through democratic norms.

Although unfolding events prevented the formation of the mass Leninist international for which Trotsky had been working (and the left-centrist organizations veered away from the fight for the Fourth International), the Trotskyist cadres were substantially strengthened by the outward-reaching orientation and by the firmer grounding in revolutionary political and organizational principles.

In the spring of 1934, Trotsky offered one of the most detailed outlines of principled democratic-centralist norms. This was in response to a crisis which had developed in the Greek section. The leader of the Greek section, Demetrious Giotopoulos, had developed disagreements with the International Secretariat of the International Communist League, and he enjoyed a majority in the section's central committee. Although not being frank about political differences, Giotopoulos began initiating a series of challenges to the authority of the International Secretariat, in preparation (as it turned out) for a break with the ICL and affiliation with the International Bureau for Revolutionary Socialist Unity (the so-called "London Bureau"—a sizeable centrist formation which included some of the elements which had recently veered away from the ILO).

Trotsky accused Giotopoulos of manifesting "the worst principles of individualism and anarchism" in his campaign against the authority of the International Secretariat, adding:

> In Greece, so far as I can judge, the majority of the Central Committee now defends and applies principles directly contrary in denying to the minority [in the Greek section] the rights and possibilities of defending openly its position before all the members of the organization. Thus individualist anarchism transforms itself into the opposite, that is, into bureaucratic centralism. (*Writings, 1933-34*, pp. 281-82)

Trotsky, utilizing Bolshevik principles to suggest a resolution to the crisis, offered the following conclusions (which constitute an outline of democratic-centralist norms):

> **a.** At the present stage of the differences, that is, insofar as they have not transcended the field of organizational conflicts, one can as yet draw conclusions neither on the depth of the differences nor on their final outcome.

b. It is therefore necessary, on one hand, to guarantee the *unity* of the organization, on the other to take all measures for a serious and honest *examination of the differences* not only in the sphere of organization but also in that of policy and program.

c. These two aims cannot be achieved otherwise than by the method of democratic centralism, that is, by means of the widest *discussion*, in a *congress convened honestly* and by *the submission of the minority to the majority*.

d. A discussion in a loyal party presupposes that the two groups *under the same conditions* submit to the knowledge of the whole party in writing and orally their points of view on the questions in dispute; every nucleus must have the possibility of having the representatives of the majority of the Central Committee as well as those of the minority of the Central Committee. It was thus and in this invariable manner that matters were arranged in the Bolshevik Party before its bureaucratic degeneration.

e. The congress of the party must be the mirror of the party. This means that from the time that a discussion bearing on platforms has surged up in the organization a congress must be convoked on the basis of *proportional representation*. This is the ABC of workers' democracy that all honest revolutionists must keep in mind.

f. Our organization is not only nominally but also in essence an international organization. That means: it places not only national discipline above local discipline but also *international discipline above national discipline*. From this follows particularly the necessity of submitting in time the theses of both groups that combat each other to all our sections to give them the opportunity to express their opinions before the congress. (*Writings, 1933-34*, p. 283)

4. The crisis of the French section

In 1934, Trotsky observed that "the unusual acuteness of the class struggle" resulted in "the tendency for reformism to be pushed aside by centrism, as well as the tendency toward the radicalization of centrism"— tendencies which he felt were increasing within the ranks of the workers' movement. The bureaucratic leaderships of the Social Democratic and Communist parties, however, were incapable of providing the necessary revolutionary leadership. While Trotsky believed that the future belonged to the yet-to-be constituted Fourth International, he pointed out: "It may be constituted in the process of the struggle against fascism and the victory gained over it. But it may also be formed considerably later, in a number of years, in the midst of the ruins and the accumulation of debris following upon the victory of fascism and war." (*Writings, 1934-35*, pp. 81, 85)

Trotsky saw the People's Front alliance of the Socialist and Communist parties of France as reflecting in some ways the working-class radicalization (the workers demanded unity to defend their rights). But he also noted that "it cannot be considered excluded that the Social Democratic bureaucracy in France, with the active aid of the Stalinists, will isolate the left wing...." (*Writings, 1934-35*, p. 83) Trotsky appreciated the contributions of the 100-member French section of the ICL but observed "that our organization is too weak to establish for itself a practical independent role in the struggles that are looming ahead of us." He urged that the section enter the French Socialist Party and constitute itself as a revolutionary faction for the purpose of escaping isolation, winning new adherents to the Bolshevik-Leninist banner (he hoped for "several thousand workers"), and becoming a significant factor in French politics. Answering objections, he explained: "...the proletarian party must be independent. Quite so. But the League is not yet a party. It is an embryo, and an embryo needs covering and nourishment in order to develop." (*Writings, 1934-35*, pp. 36, 38, 43)

At first, there was considerable opposition within the French section to this proposal. In the autumn of 1934, however, it decided to implement this proposal, which came to be known as "the French turn." By the summer of 1935 it had (within the Socialist Party) 300 members, tens of thousands of readers of its press, and significant influence in the larger organization and—through this—in other sectors of the workers' movement. Within a short period of time, the leadership of the Socialist Party launched a campaign to curb and, ultimately, to eliminate the revolutionary threat within the party's ranks.

Trotsky now called for a new turn:

> This party opened to us certain possibilities, and it was correct to have formulated and utilized them. But these possibilities are limited. The Mulhouse Congress [of the Socialist Party, at which the Trotskyists won support from a sizeable minority for a revolutionary anti-militarist resolution, and became nationally prominent for their vigorous challenge to the Socialist leadership], together with the repercussions that will follow it, should more or less materially limit these possibilities. The prestige gained by the Bolshevik-Leninist Group must transform itself by flooding light upon the workers.... The inevitable regroupment in the different working-class organizations (Communist Party, trade unions, etc.) must open for us an outlet to the working class masses. It is necessary to

orient ourselves in this direction with all the required independence.... It is absolutely essential to speed up the preparatory work
for the Fourth International. (*Writings, 1934-35*, pp. 317-18)

The leadership of the French section—already beset by organizational
inexperience, severe personality conflicts, feuds and cliques—was divided
over how quickly, how, *or even if* they should leave the Socialist Party. Splits
resulted which consumed considerable time and energy. At times, certain elements recklessly flouted the authority and decisions of the international
and national organizations. A unified and independent section, however,
was finally achieved in June 1936, with a membership of over 600. The
French police warned the government that the reorganized group had the
potential to become a formidable force. But over the next four months, sav-
age in-fighting in the organization reduced the membership by almost one-
fourth. This debacle occurred during the most massive labor upsurge in
French history—upon which the French section had little impact. A police
report in September noted: "Because of its internal struggles and the sectarianism of its militants...it can be affirmed today that this group for the moment is incapable of provoking and leading any kind of social movement."
In October, another split devastated the organization. Although fragments
continued to exist and eventually reorganized, they had to do so "in the
midst of the ruins and accumulation of debris following upon the victory
of fascism and war." (*Crisis of the French Section*, pp. 136, 165)

In these complex and tragic events were many rich lessons on organizational principles, and Trotsky sought to draw attention to them. What
follows are some of his many comments on: a) principled politics, b) democratic centralism, c) party-building, d) the need to turn to mass struggles
and the working class.

a) Principled politics

In the autumn of 1935, Trotsky commented to a young comrade: "You
know, there isn't much choice! You have to work with the material that you
have on hand." He was speaking of the membership of the Trotskyist movement, with all of the individual comrades' limitations. He went on to say that
a certain "spark" was very important: "the desire to act, the struggle with one's
face bare, to assert oneself and, if necessary, to sacrifice everything to the independence of one's ideas." Revolutionary will is necessary but insufficient
for consistent revolutionary work, however, for "quite often revolutionary
impatience...becomes transformed easily into opportunist impatience...."
A necessary supplement to this "spark"—something which is ultimately nec-

essary to keep the spark alive—is revolutionary theory: "To the degree that you have a clear theoretical vision of things, you will also have the political will to put it into effect." (*Crisis of the French Section*, pp. 67, 72, 97)

"To make concessions of principle…would only mean undermining our own future," Trotsky warned. For example, the entry into the French Socialist Party did not in any way mean "sheathing the banner of Marxism"—and

> to renounce the principles or to "provisionally" relinquish the struggle for them would be open treason. But to bring the methods of struggle in congruence with the situation and our own forces is an elementary demand of Bolshevism…. Naturally the League cannot enter the Socialist Party other than as a Bolshevik-Leninist faction. (*Crisis of the French Section*, pp. 76, 43, 42)

Similarly, Trotsky argued that concessions could not be made for the purposes of remaining inside of (or "making gains" in) the Socialist Party. Trotsky further explained this by referring to the question of tone.

> There is the question of our *political line*. It must be directed toward independence [from the reformism of the Socialist Party], which is dictated by the whole situation, above all by the conscious will of our enemies…. But there is also the *tactical* and *pedagogical* question. This has its own rights and obligations which—in the final analysis, of course—are subordinate to our political line. (*Crisis of the French Section*, p. 54)

Trotsky added:

> If all the good comrades in our ranks understood the depth of our differences [with the reformists and centrists], then they will also have to understand that the *tone* of the polemic must correspond to the sharpness of the differences. Otherwise, the workers would believe that it is a matter of secondary differences within the same family. Marxism comports itself here in an irreconcilable manner toward right-leaning centrism. This means a fight to the finish, without considerations of tact. (*Crisis of the French Section*, pp. 57-8)

"Good intentions, however indisputable, are not enough," Trotsky concluded. "They must be guided by correct principles and controlled by a cohesive organization." (*Crisis of the French Section*, p. 118)

b) Democratic centralism

"Centralism means focusing the maximum organizational effort toward the 'goal.' It is the only means of leading millions of people in combat against the possessing classes," Trotsky explained.

If we agree with Lenin, that we are in the epoch of imperialism, the last stage of capitalism, it is necessary to have a revolutionary organization flexible enough to deal with the problems of an underground struggle as well as those of the seizure of power. Hence the necessity of a strongly centralized party, capable of orienting and leading the masses and of conducting the gigantic struggle from which they should emerge victorious. Hence also the need to collectively make a loyal self-criticism at every stage. (*Crisis of the French Section*, p. 68)

At the same time, he stressed: "The Fourth International will not tolerate mechanical 'monolithism' in its ranks. On the contrary, one of its most important tasks is to regenerate on a new, higher historical plane the 'revolutionary democracy of the proletarian vanguard.'" He pointed out: "The principle of Bolshevik organization is 'democratic centralism,' assured by complete freedom of criticism and of groupings, together with steel discipline in action. The history of the party is at the same time the history of the internal struggle of ideas, groupings, factions." (*Crisis of the French Section*, p. 47)

There was, however, a particular kind of grouping which Trotsky found fitted in poorly with a revolutionary party, in spite of democratic-centralist norms: the clique. He believed that a clique gathered around one of its central leaders, Raymond Molinier, had done considerable damage within the French section. "The M. clique has changed its position ten times over. I refer to this as a 'personal clique' in the Marxist sense of the term, a grouping which surrounds an individual and covers for all his misdeeds despite numerous changes in political position." After a seven-year experience with Molinier, Trotsky concluded: "The very fact that the whole organization is obliged at every instant to occupy itself with R.M. and not with questions that are infinitely more important shows the incompatibility of R.M. with the revolutionary organization." (*Crisis of the French Section*, pp. 156, 152)

Trotsky was particularly incensed with the Molinier group's maneuvering around the decisions—at times even outright violation of decisions—of the party and international leadership. Trotsky protested that "he is making a joke of the formal decisions of, the obligations undertaken by, and the public opinion of our international organization, as well as of the national section." Trotsky took this opportunity to repeat: "International discipline prevails in every case over national discipline." It is worth noting that, in Trotsky's opinion, a national leadership has no right to impose discipline on the rank-and-file if the leadership itself was violating international discipline and basic principles: "They have no right to demand discipline, since they have broken with the international organization and renounced the most fundamental principles, which is much more important." (*Crisis of the French Section*, pp. 151-52, 96, 142)

All of this obviously raises important questions about the relation of the party's internal regime to correct methods of party building.

c) Party building and responsibilities of leadership

Trotsky believed that the leadership of a revolutionary organization has immense responsibilities. One of these is the maintenance of a healthy party atmosphere:

> …it is always necessary to see to it that the atmosphere remains healthy and the internal climate acceptable to everyone. Comrades should work with all their heart and with the maximum of confidence.
>
> Building the revolutionary party requires patience and hard work. At any price, the best should not be discouraged, and you should show yourselves capable of working with everyone. Each person is a lever to be fully utilized to strengthen the party. Lenin knew the art of doing that. After the liveliest, most polemical discussions, he knew how to find the words and the gestures that would soften unfortunate or offensive remarks. (*Crisis of the French Section*, p. 70)

As the class struggle accelerated in 1936, Trotsky wrote hopefully to the Political Bureau of the French section: "Under the pressure of great events one learns quickly. What is needed now is a *firm nucleus* in the leadership capable of making decisions, giving directives, and place the 'freelancers,' adventurers, and factionalists in a position where they can do no harm." In the previous year he had described the functioning of the Bolshevik party leadership in similar terms: "Between congresses, it was the Central Committee and its Political Bureau that led the party and supervised the rigorous execution at every level of the policy decided by the majority. It was not permissible to return constantly to questions of orientation and thus to violate the execution of the policy decided on by the party." (*Crisis of the French Section*, pp. 153, 69)

Taking the leadership of the organization so seriously, Trotsky was shocked by a decision of the French section to hold Central Committee meetings that were open to the entire membership:

I confess, I cannot understand this at all. The Central Committee is the revolutionary general staff. How can it sit publicly? You must have in the organization a serious percentage of police agents, Stalinists, GPU agents, etc. These will be the first visitors to the Central Committee. At every session of the Central Committee there are secret or confidential questions. There is the need to discipline different comrades, etc. To have a little "gallery" for the sessions means to *hinder* the normal work of the leading body."

Yet he certainly didn't see the leadership as being in any way autonomous, for in the next breath he was adding: "The organization must have the opportunity to control its leaders and their methods. It is the only way to prepare a good selection of comrades for the leadership." (*Crisis of the French Section*, pp. 146, 147)

Trotsky was quite serious about the need to control the party leadership. "France's development in the coming period will be very rich in crises," he wrote in June 1936, "and each turning point within the crisis can bring about opportunist or adventurist reactions within the leading layer of the French section." How could such problems in the leadership be overcome? "Through active supervision by the ranks, that is, by members of the French section, and through equally active supervision by our international organization." In this way, the membership also bears responsibility for the internal regime—and all of this obviously reflects Trotsky's conception of democratic centralism. He rejoiced when it appeared "that the rank and file is at last beginning to occupy itself with surveillance of the leadership. This is a necessary condition for the cohesiveness of the organization." (*Crisis of the French Section*, pp. 141, 142, 151)

Trotsky especially felt that the leadership must raise the level of professionalism in the organization: "If you do not train good, serious administrators at every level of the movement, you will not win even if you are right a thousand times over. What the Bolshevik-Leninists have always lacked—and particularly in France—are organizers, good treasurers, accurate accounting, and publications that are readable and well proofread." Trotsky also insisted that party perspectives must be based on "facts throwing light on the real situation and not of general formulas that might be applied equally well to Paris or Honolulu." In line with this, he urged:

It is necessary to organize an information service: newspaper clippings, letters, reports, personal reports, etc. It is necessary for someone to make it his business to tirelessly classify documents, to study them, to trace the curve of the movement, etc. This is the only way to keep our fingers on the pulse of the working class. It is also the only means of building up the different departments of the "general headquarters." (*Crisis of the French Section*, pp. 68, 155; *Writings, 1934-35*, p. 58)

The leadership also bears responsibility for offering realistic projections for practical work:

> Do only what you are able to do with the forces at your disposal. Never more, except, of course, in decisive situations.... Whatever you do, set yourself an objective, even if very modest, but strive to attain it. Proceed this way in every phase of organization. Then you should elaborate a short- or long-term plan. That is the only way to move forward and make the whole organization progress. (*Crisis of the French Section*, p. 71)

Trotsky stressed the importance of "menial daily work" (such as circulation of the party press), explaining: "The revolutionary movement is composed of dozens of just such 'uninteresting,' 'technical' labors. Without detailed and assiduous preparatory work it is impossible to begin with a militia or a strike, and even less so with the general strike or the insurrection." (*Writings, 1934-35*, p. 34)

Leaders of the organization should be concerned, also, about strengthening "the fraternal bonds among the comrades in struggle." Trotsky explained:

> It is necessary to preserve, encourage, and watch over those bonds. An experienced worker member represents an inestimable *capital* for the organization. It takes years to educate a leader. We therefore should do everything possible to save a member. Don't destroy him if he weakens, but help him to overcome his weakness, to get over his moment of doubt.
>
> Never forget those who "fall" by the wayside. Help them to return to the organization if you have nothing irremediable to reproach them for on the level of revolutionary morality. (*Crisis of the French Section*, pp. 69-70)

Trotsky suggested ways of leadership functioning that would maximize the development of comrades:

> Leave maximum initiative to the responsible comrades in their own field. If errors are committed, correct them by explaining in a comradely fashion how they are harmful to the party as a whole. Do not take administrative measures except in unusually serious cases. As a general rule everyone should be allowed to advance, develop, and improve. (*Crisis of the French Section*, p. 69)

Trotsky was concerned with the development of a particular kind of political skill within the Trotskyist movement:

> Theoretical routine, this absence of political and tactical creativity, is no substitute for perspicacity, an ability to size things up at a glance, the flair for "feeling" a situation while sorting out the main threads and developing an over-all strategy. In a revolutionary and especially an insurrectional period these qualities become decisive. (*Crisis of the French Section*, p. 69)

The development of this revolutionary-activist "flair" presupposes, of course, involvement in mass political work and the class struggle.

d) The turn to workers and mass struggles

Trotsky pointed out that "the [French Communist] League (like other sections) was forced to develop as an isolated propaganda group. This determined both its positive sides (an honest and serious attachment to the principles) and its negative sides (observing the labor movement from the outside)." He fought to overcome the negative: "It is particularly now [1934] that we must put up a pitiless fight against abstract, passive propagandism, against a policy of waiting." Polemicizing against those inclined to abstain from the actual struggles, he complained: "These comrades substitute a monologue for actual political work among the masses. Their politics follows the line of least resistance; it is politics of self-complacency disguised by formulas of imaginary intransigence." (*Writings, 1934-35*, pp. 33, 60, 59) Trotsky explained:

> The revolutionary ideas must be transformed into life itself every day through the experience of the masses themselves. But how can the League explain this to them when it is itself cut off from the experience of the masses? It is necessary to add: several comrades do not even see the need of this experience. It seems to them to be sufficient to form an opinion on the basis of newspaper accounts they read and then to give it expression in an article or talk. Yet if the most correct ideas do not reflect directly the ideas and actions of the mass, they will escape the attention of the masses altogether. (*Writings, 1934-35*, p. 34)

Trotsky reemphasized this point again and again. "All his life Lenin fought against sectarian deviations that will and have cut revolutionaries off from mass movements and from a clear understanding of the situation." (*Crisis of the French Section*, p. 69) He urged his comrades more deeply to penetrate the ranks of the Socialist workers, not in order to 'lecture' down to them from above as learned specialists in strategy, but in order to learn together with the advanced workers, shoulder to shoulder, on the basis of actual mass experience, which will inevitably lead the French proletariat on the road of revolutionary struggle. (*Writings, 1934-35*, p. 50)

5. Crises of the American section

From the moment when Trotsky first established contact with his American co-thinkers in 1929 until his death in 1940, Trotsky frequently and freely offered his advice and guidance on political questions. Not the least of these involved important organizational questions confronting the American section. In the process he applied many of the organizational principles already discussed. Also contained in his writings on the organizational problems of the American section are many new insights on such questions as the nature of democratic centralism, how a good leadership functions, and guidelines for minority tendencies and factions in the revolutionary party. This section will chronologically review some of Trotsky's more important contributions to the discussion of organizational questions in the American section.

a) Averting an unprincipled split

In the early 1930s a faction fight divided the young Communist League of America with a majority led by James P. Cannon and Arne Swabeck and a minority led by Max Shachtman, Martin Abern, and Albert Glotzer. By 1932-33 the fight had brought the CLA to the verge of a split. Arne Swabeck visited Trotsky in Turkey in early 1933 in an attempt to win Trotsky's support to the majority faction. As Swabeck described the situation there were no questions of principle on which the two factions disagreed. Rather, the political questions in dispute were "of what conception one has of a communist organization. What methods should be employed?" (*Supplement, 1929-33*, p. 195) He depicted the minority as advocating methods that would continue to restrict the CLA's activities to literary ones, while the majority wanted more participation in the class struggle. Also, the minority had opposed sending Swabeck as the CLA's official representative to the preconference of the International Left Opposition, which was held in France in February 1933.

When the majority had asked if the minority wanted its own representative at the preconference, the minority demanded that a national conference be convened immediately. Swabeck explained to Trotsky that the majority was not against a conference, but wanted ample time to discuss national and international questions in depth. The two factions also had disagreed over whether or not Max Eastman should be allowed to participate in a public meeting to answer Stalinist slanders. And, finally, Swabeck complained that Shachtman "viewed everything as a personal question" and that in editing *The Militant* he "keeps the comrades waiting, and edits the paper in a far too individualistic fashion." (*Supplement, 1929-34*, p. 199)

Differences had also arisen over internal organizational questions. At the June 1932 plenum of the National Committee, the majority proposed that three additional majority supporters be co-opted onto the National Committee in order to strengthen its position on the NC resident committee in New York. Initially, the minority agreed, but later reversed its position and the co-optation was rejected in a national referendum vote. The majority contended that the New York branch, which supported the NC minority, was not proletarian enough. To correct this, the majority proposed that only workers be accepted as new members for a six-month period and that all members be obliged to actively participate and report on their activities in a mass organization. The minority, in combination with another grouping, opposed the resolution and it was defeated.

On Swabeck's departure for Europe to participate in the preconference, he had suggested that Cannon be assigned to take his place as national secretary. The minority rejected this and argued instead for a secretariat of two comrades, Cannon and Abern. Swabeck further charged that the minority had joined in unprincipled blocs with other CLA groupings in order to oppose criticism of members for direct violations of discipline. And in April/May 1932 the minority had begun to work as an organized faction with its own center, finances, etc. But since there were no major political differences and the minority had not put out its own platform, Swabeck argued that the minority faction had no principled basis.

Trotsky gave his evaluation of the situation in the conversation with Swabeck and later in a series of letters to Swabeck, Shachtman, and Glotzer. Trotsky basically accepted Swabeck's assessment that the fundamental source of the problem in the CLA was in the different traditions of the two main factions and in the heterogeneity of the League's social composition, coupled with the new organizational tasks of the League:

> I have only been able to determine that the majority of the central committee consists of comrades who are, so to speak, more American, who were involved in revolutionary organizations even before

the advent of the Communist Party, in the IWW, while the leaders of the minority are younger comrades who haven't worked in the unions and the revolutionary organizations. The other point is that according to Comrade Swabeck's reports the workers in the local organizations, especially those with trade union experience, tend to go with the majority, while the intellectuals, etc., who have come to the organization more or less on an ideological basis, go with the minority. This division is not absolutely accurate, but is more or less correct. It is important insofar as it corresponds to the facts for there are certain socially based points of support. Since the organization was oriented more toward propaganda work, this can account for the fact that these differences or divergencies, which are based in the social composition of the organization, have not yet broken through to the surface. Up till now, for both groups, it has been a question of finding the correct propaganda formulations, and since the different compositions of the two groups and the different traditions (or in the one case—the absence of traditions) have not yet found political expression, they are channeled, so to speak, into side roads—into organizational and personal questions, etc. That is what is most dangerous. (*Supplement, 1929-33*, p. 199)

Yet these factors in themselves did not necessitate a split—particularly if the League successfully managed to direct its efforts outward. Trotsky noted:

The very fact that the two factions have different social compositions and different traditions is not sufficient to make a split necessary, for every party is formed from different groups, elements, etc., and is not socially homogeneous. And every party is a melting pot, but there has to be activity. The present situation in the League will become a melting pot. To a certain extent this is dependent on opportunities and successes. If you score successes, this will weld together the best elements. In case of failures and inch-by-inch development, the discontent can find its expression in a split. (*Supplement, 1929-33*, pp. 199-200)

Trotsky emphasized the importance of the party's turning outward, and its interrelationship with the party's internal life:

Not convincing, it seems to me, is the allegation that in spite of the hopes of any 'optimists' the situation became even more acute after the League began to pass from the propaganda to the agitation stage. It is by passing from one stage into another that the malady usually comes to the surface. But serious successes in the field of mass work will inevitably produce a favorable influence upon internal relations and in every case provoke a radical regroupment by gradual isolation of demoralized elements. (*Supplement, 1929-33*, p. 213)

In such circumstances, with political ideas so ill-defined, Trotsky strongly opposed the perspective of a split. As Trotsky explained to Swabeck: "A split would destroy the League and compromise the movement seriously. One cannot explain a split to the workers by unclear social stratifications on the one hand and the expression that these find in organizational and political forms on the other." (*Supplement, 1929-33*, p. 200)

And he insisted on the same point to minority leaders, writing to Glotzer: "…a split without a clear political character is the most dangerous kind of miscarriage, one which can kill both the mother and the child." (*Supplement, 1929-33*, p. 217)

In light of the disastrous consequences of such a split, Trotsky turned his attention to the subjective sources of the intensity of the differences within the CLA. As Trotsky characterized the solution to the situation, the political immaturity of the organization was responsible:

> When an organization is politically mature and its members have experience in factional struggle, the frictions can be held in check until the major political differences are evident. However, the debates often appear to be purely personal and organizational. The special nature of the situation consists in the fact that the intensity of the struggle does not correspond to the stage of development in the formation of factions. Both factions find themselves, so to speak, in a state of infancy, they have no clearly developed form. On the other hand, they are already organized as factions and confront the League more or less with a split. And that can destroy it. When a split takes place after intense political struggles, it can be understandable and natural. But the way things stand in the League, I believe there is also an element of personal fault involved. (*Supplement, 1929-33*, pp. 200-01)

In an effort to forestall a split Trotsky cautioned restraint on both sides. To Swabeck, representing the majority, Trotsky emphasized the responsibility of the majority for the intensity of the factional struggle: "The fact that the conflict has flared up so prematurely and with such intensity, and that no one knows how to cool it down—that seems to me to be a negative symptom for the leadership." (*Supplement, 1929-33*, p. 201)

He further remarked:

> After having a series of discussions with you and becoming acquainted with the [CLA] documents, I think—entirely apart from any assessment of the minority's attitude—that in the organizational policy of the majority of the central committee there are elements of formal intransigence which may appear as bureaucratism

and which in any case will injure rather than enhance the authority of the central committee and its influence.... The Oppositional minority has a certain right to manifest impatience but the majority leadership has no such right. (*Supplement, 1929-33,* pp. 212-13)

On the other hand, in letters to the minority, Trotsky emphasized the minority's responsibility. To Shachtman he wrote: "I would really like to implore you, as well as your friends, not to be so nervous, so impatient, to adopt a longer-range perspective and not for a moment to forget that we have an international organization that is not at all inclined to adopt a one-sided view and in whose eyes the 'aggressor,' the instigator, has much more to lose than to win." (*Supplement, 1929-33,* p. 214)

Similarly, he advised Glotzer: "Do not in any case or under any circumstances exacerbate the situation in the League.... Any impatience on the part of your group would make a split very likely.... Patience, dear Glotzer, you must prepare yourself for long-term work." (*Supplement, 1929-33,* p. 217)

With regard to specific differences, Trotsky focused on the errors of the majority while addressing Swabeck, and the errors of the minority in his correspondence with Shachtman and Glotzer. To Swabeck, Trotsky condemned the majority's position on a whole series of questions. First, regarding the question of the co-optation on the National Committee, Trotsky doubted this necessity. (*Cooptation* means the leadership appointing an additional person or additional people to a leadership body rather than making such an addition through elections within the organization as a whole.) Trotsky thought such an action by the majority would appear to members as undemocratic and factionally motivated, and characterized this move as evidence of "organizational intolerance." He reviewed:

Let's take the question of cooptation, for instance: Comrade Swabeck himself recognizes that this measure did not benefit the popularity of the leadership. I wonder if the results really justify this measure. The figures are very interesting: the members of the local organizations see that all resolutions have been adopted unanimously and a proposal is made for cooptations in order to reinforce the 'majority.' The members ask themselves: 'What majority? You have been able to clarify your standpoint so that the minority has been forced to follow suit.' The cooptation proposal has caused dissatisfaction among the membership. On the one hand, they see it as undemocratic, on the other, as factional, as dangerous for the unity of the organization. So there were very good reasons motivating the no vote. The membership does not want a leadership artificially imposed upon it and, secondly, it has good enough reasons to be concerned about the organization. The result was the vote against the majority and the shaking of the majority's position despite the fact that it wished to strengthen its position. It was an inappropriate measure and revealed perhaps too much organizational intolerance. Given the present situation, it would perhaps be better in the long run not to carry out cooptations. (*Supplement, 1929-33*, p. 201)

Trotsky further remarked: "In order to justify the cooptation you would have had to propose a resolution that forced the minority to vote against it. That would have made the emergency measures clear to the organization. But perhaps such a course of action was impossible since there were no such deepgoing differences of opinion, and that very fact made the cooptation an arbitrary measure." (*Supplement, 1929-33*, p. 203)

On the question of national secretary, the question of the central leadership position in the organization, Trotsky argued that the majority position exacerbated differences, and he proposed a compromise:

> Of course it was quite natural to propose Cannon as secretary, but perhaps in Cannon's position I would say: "I would like a representative of the minority to work with me as assistant secretary." That would be an attempt to cooperatively regulate the disputed questions and perhaps the frictions would indeed be lessened in the course of day-to-day collaboration. The personal-organizational disputes are out of proportion to the stage of maturation of the principled differences. It seems to me that in fact an element of organizational "ultimatism" on the part of the majority played a role. (*Supplement, 1929-33*, pp. 201-02)

In fact, Trotsky noted, "In consideration of the fact that the two groups have approximately the same weight it would be, it seems to me, reasonable for the majority to make a concession to the minority and after the designation of Comrade Cannon as permanent secretary to draw in also Comrade Abern as assistant secretary." (*Supplement, 1929-33*, p. 212)

Under the circumstances, Trotsky opposed the majority proposal for the proletarianization of the New York branch: "The proposal of the central committee to the New York branch concerning proletarianization was a mistake not in its general tendency but in its mechanical approach to the issue and the manifestly practical hopelessness of the proposal under the given conditions." (*Supplement, 1929-33*, p. 212)

In his letter to Swabeck, Trotsky also opposed the factionally-motivated proposals by the majority to deprive Abern of his vote on the resident committee of the National Committee while Swabeck was in Europe, the drafting and circulating to foreign comrades of theses on American imperialism behind the backs of the minority, and the majority proposal to transfer the national headquarters to Chicago.

At the same time, writing to Shachtman and Glotzer, Trotsky criticized the protests of the minority against sending Swabeck to Europe for the pre-conference and to visit Trotsky.

Finally, Trotsky explained to both groups that neither side could gain substantially from a victory at the national conference of the CLA scheduled for June-July 1933. And if the faction with a small majority at the conference attempted to use their victory to change everything in the party, a split would ensue and members would be lost. He explained to Swabeck:

> The third conference in June-July: In the present situation what can it accomplish? Perhaps it can adopt good resolutions, but as far as the disputes between the different groupings are concerned we can say: 110 here and 100 there or the other way around. Everything will be as before. The majority stands only to lose, since it cannot hope to win eight seats as against one for the minority. In such a situation personal relations play a very great role. Naturally, if one says the split is unavoidable, I have my 51 percent, I am going to set a course for throwing the others out—this can be carried through to the end. But there must be *political reasons* for it.... We must express this perspective very clearly: what do the comrades hope to gain from a new conference and what can they hope to gain—110 to 100? If you chart a course toward establishing a majority of a few percent on one side and then changing everything, then you will just lose members, because immediately an element will appear which heads for the sidelines. (*Supplement, 1929-33*, p. 202)

In the same vein, Trotsky wrote to Shachtman: "In one of your letters you gave expression to the hope that the next conference will settle the disputes. That is not my opinion at all. If your group gets 51 percent that would not change anything at all." (*Supplement, 1929-33*, p. 214)

And to Glotzer he wrote,

> It also seems to me that it is wrong to hope for a national convention that will 'put everything right.' Under present circumstances the convention could only bring about an unimportant shift in the relationship of forces. Whether your group has five and the other group four on the central committee, or the other way around, is rather unimportant since each group is dependent on the other if things are not to be driven to a split, i.e., a catastrophe. (*Supplement, 1929-33*, p. 217)

Besides appealing to both sides for restraint, Trotsky requested the "determined intervention" of the International Secretariat of the ILO in order to prevent a split. With the aid of Trotsky and the International Secretariat, a truce was accepted by both sides in the spring of 1933 and a split was averted. Under the joint leadership of Cannon and Shachtman, the American section thrived and became a significant revolutionary force during the next six years.

b) Against freelancing

At the beginning of 1934 a unionizing drive developed among the hotel workers in New York City. In the course of the movement, an intellectual named B. J. Field was assigned by the League to help the CLA's hotel union fraction and to assist the union. Largely because of Field's knowledge of French, the French chefs in the union insisted that Field become the new secretary of the union. The movement quickly grew into a general strike of the New York hotel workers. Simultaneously, the growth of Field's ego paralleled the growth of the strike. Soon he was spending all of his time meeting with politicians and labor bureaucrats. But he could find no time to consult with the National Committee of the CLA about the policy of the strike.

Meanwhile, the strike began to suffer as a result of misleadership. Field was moderating the militancy of the workers while wasting time in negotiations with Mayor Fiorello La Guardia. By his actions Field was not only weakening the strike, but also compromising the name of the CLA. The leadership of the CLA finally concluded that decisive action was necessary. In the middle of the strike Field was put on trial for violating party discipline. Field and his supporters who refused to submit to discipline were expelled.

Soon after Field's expulsion, Trotsky wrote to Field, disagreeing with his views and affirming the right of the CLA to control the political activities of its members:

> …The [Communist] League is, however, the nucleus of the new
> party and thereby of the new international. To me it seems completely unforgivable to break with one's own organization at the
> first practical test. Your explanations for this are unfortunately full
> of contradictions. In discussing the NC's reorganization of the
> [League's hotel union] fraction, you say there are no political reasons for the artificial differences of opinion. But then you maintain
> that the League is sectarian, sterile, incapable of mass action, and
> even dead. If in your opinion the League is dead, the break with the
> corpse is understandable. This means however that you are breaking with our movement. But since the League does not regard itself

as dead—and I believe rightly so—it cannot allow its members to freelance. Rather it wishes to exercise control over its members. If it had not desired this, it would not be worthy of existence.

In the Social Democratic parties, it was and still is the rule that when gifted members of the party with the party's help win important posts in the municipality, the parliament, or the ministry, they immediately become tired of party discipline and declare that the official leadership of the party is incompetent in order to carry out their own political line—always in order to "save" the party, of course. (*Supplement, 1934-40*, pp. 462-63)

c) The sectarian opposition

During the summer of 1934, Trotsky proposed to the French Trotskyists that they enter the French Socialist Party. Applying an analogous policy to the United States, the CLA leadership proposed a fusion with the American Workers Party (AWP)—the organization politically closest to the CLA and moving to the left. In October 1934 the plenum of the International Communist League approved the turn in France, which soon afterwards also was applied in other countries as a means of turning the ICL from a propaganda circle to mass work.

As we have seen, the turn was not effected without opposition in the French section. In the United States a group in the CLA led by Hugo Oehler also objected to the turn. Though the Oehlerites had many reservations about the fusion with the AWP, they did not directly oppose it. But they saw any fusion with a section of the Second International as a betrayal of principle, arguing that the Second International had proven itself to be totally reformist and bankrupt at the outset of World War I and that unconditional independence was a fundamental principle of a revolutionary party.

Cannon, Shachtman and other leaders of the CLA countered the arguments of the Oehlerites by pointing out that the Second International was not the same organization it had been in 1914. A whole new generation of healthy worker militants had joined since then. And though it was true that independence is a principle for a revolutionary party, the ICL was not yet a party, but a propaganda group.

Differences came to a head after the formation of the Workers Party of the United States in December 1934 through the fusion of the CLA and the AWP. At the June plenum in 1935 the Cannon-Shachtman group proposed that the Workers Party devote more attention to the Socialist Party, leaving organizational perspectives open for the time being. In reply the Oehlerites demanded a permanent renunciation of the perspective of entry with the SP. Also, they falsely accused the Cannon-Shachtman group of attempting to maneuver the party into an SP entry behind the backs of the membership. The June plenum closed with the Cannon-Shachtman group in a minority. But during several months of extensive discussion among the ranks, the Oehlerites found themselves increasingly isolated. At that point they began to violate discipline, circulating their own publications at public meetings in spite of prohibitions by the party. Furthermore, they demanded the right to set up their own independent press. The October 1935 plenum rejected the Oehlerite demands and warned them to cease their violations of party discipline. But they continued and were expelled not long after the October plenum.

During the fight with the Oehlerites, Trotsky polemicized sharply against the sectarianism of their views. But he also denounced their methods. When the Oehlerites began to accuse Cannon and Shachtman of conspiring behind the back of the party with leaders of the SP, Trotsky warned of the consequences of such accusations:

> I had read with attention the minutes of your plenum and with a certain horror I have read of your Control Commission. One seems to breathe in a somewhat nightmarish atmosphere when one reads of the suspicions and rumors directed against comrades who have long fought for the ideas of the proletarian revolutionary struggle. Such methods can paralyze and demoralize the party unless they are at once brought to an end by the will of all. (*Writings, 1935-36*, p. 172)

And Trotsky traced the origin of such behavior to the sectarianism of the Oehlerites:

> How does it happen that Comrades Oehler, Stamm, and others take recourse to such means? We have had in France an analogous case with Bauer, who, not content with a political struggle against the 'turn,' suddenly became an inexhaustible source of suspicions, accusations, and even unbelievable slanders directed against all of us. He was, however, an honest and sincere man, devoted to socialism. His misfortune is that he is a sick sectarian. Such a man can remain tranquil and friendly so long as the life of the organization continues to revolve in familiar circles. But woe be it if events bring about a radical change! The sectarian no longer recognizes his world. All reality stands marshaled against him and, since the facts flout him, he turns his back on them and comforts himself with rumors, suspicions, and fantasies. He thus becomes a source of slanders with-

out being by nature a slanderer. He is not dishonest. He is simply in irreconcilable conflict with reality. (*Writings, 1935-36*, pp. 72-73)

Trotsky conceded the possibility that the Cannon group had too quickly resorted to organizational measures against Oehler. And he urged the party to correct the leadership on this if it was true:

> Comrades Weber and Glotzer accuse the Cannon group of pro-ceeding too rudely and bureaucratically against Oehler. I cannot express an opinion on this charge, since I have not had the oppor-tunity to follow the development of the struggle. *Hypothetically*, I can concede the possibility of a certain hastiness on the part of the leading comrades. It would naturally be a mistake to desire to or-ganizationally liquidate an opposition group before the over-whelming majority of the party has had the chance to fully understand the inconsistency and sterility of that group. Leaders are often impatient in seeking to remove an obstacle in the path of the party's activity. In such cases the party can and must correct the precipitateness of the leaders, since it is not only the leaders who educate the party but also the party that educates the leaders. Herein lies the salutary dialectic of democratic centralism. (*Writ-ings, 1935-36*, p. 73)

However Trotsky believed it was mistaken to view Cannon's errors as equal to Oehler's when it was precisely Oehlerite sectarianism that threat-ened the life of the Workers Party:

> Comrades Weber and Glotzer are decidedly wrong when they place on the same plane the "mistakes" of Oehler and the mistakes of Cannon. Sectarianism is a cancer which threatens the activity of the WP, which paralyzes it, envenoms discussions, and prevents coura-geous steps forward in the life of the workers' organizations. I should like to hope that a surgical operation will not be necessary. But precisely in order to avoid expulsions, it is necessary to strike pitilessly at the Oehler group by a decision of an overwhelming ma-jority. This is the preliminary condition of all possible future suc-cesses for the Workers Party. We all want it to remain independent, but before all and above all, independent of the cancer which is eat-ing at its vitals. (*Writings, 1935-36*, p. 73)

Even while denouncing their views and methods, Trotsky offered to Oehlerites the prospect of reconciliation:

> Oehlerite comrades! Carry out a turn of 180 degrees in your atti-tude on the French question! Get to work to tell the American workers of the courage and devotion with which the Bolshevik-Leninists of France are conducting their struggle. We will gladly

forget unmerited reproaches and false accusations. You will again
find your place of combat in our international ranks. But if you
persist in your completely untenable attitude, you will be lost for a
long time to come for the revolutionary movement. (*Writings,
1935-36*, pp. 77-78)

As we have seen, however, Trotsky's appeals to the Oehlerites were unsuc-
cessful.

In December 1935 a split occurred in the Socialist Party of America, re-
moving most of that party's right wing. Cannon and Shachtman saw an
opportunity for the Workers Party in this and in January 1936 proposed
that members of the Workers Party join the SP. A national convention on
this question was called for late February. Even though the Oehlerites had
been expelled, there remained a significant minority in the Workers Party
who opposed entering the SP on tactical grounds. Trotsky immediately en-
dorsed the proposal for entry. He explained that the greatest gain would be
in helping to resolve the crisis that had afflicted the Workers Party for so
many months. (For example, see *Writings, 1935-36*, p. 260)

Subsequently, the February convention authorized entry into the SP.
The minority leaders announced "their loyal support of the decision
adopted," and the crisis in the Workers Party was overcome. In March, the
Workers Party members began joining SP branches. And in June 1935 the
Workers Party was formally dissolved.

d) Building the Socialist Workers Party

The Trotskyists remained within the Socialist Party for over a year.
During that time they made impressive gains, most importantly, drawing
around themselves the most serious and militant of the young workers in
the SP and a majority of the SP's youth affiliate. Largely due to their successes, the wing of the SP leadership influenced by Stalinism and the wing
gravitating towards the Democratic Party united to drive the Trotskyists
out of the SP. Through the summer of 1937 they conducted wholesale ex-
pulsions of the Trotskyists. Finally, at the start of 1938, Trotskyists reconsti-
tuted themselves as a party—the Socialist Workers Party. Among the
successes of the previous year and a half was the fact that they had more
than doubled their membership.

Trotsky was closely watching these developments and advising the
comrades as they began to move toward reconstituting themselves as an independent party in late 1937. He repeatedly stressed that in the coming period the emphasis in the new party must be placed on democracy, not

centralism. Trotsky saw this as necessary in order to carry out the training and assimilation of the many new members just recruited in the SP as well as those the SWP hoped and expected to recruit in the near future. Thus, he wrote to Cannon in September 1936:

> Our organization will become attractive to very different people in the next period, and not only for the best of them. Public life in the States is very agitated, and the recent announcement of the new crisis will aggravate the disquietude, the fighting spirit, and…the confusion. We can't avoid having this confusion in our ranks. Our comrades are "too" educated, "too" accustomed to precise, elaborated conceptions and slogans. They have a contempt for everybody who is not ideologically "O.K." It is very dangerous. A developing and alive party must represent—to a certain extent—the different tendencies, disquietudes and, I repeat, even the confusion in the vanguard of the working class. Too much confusion is, of course, not good but a sound proportion can be established only through practice. More pedagogical patience is absolutely necessary on the part of our comrades toward the new and fresh elements. That is the genuine meaning of party 'democracy.' I believe that for the next period the emphasis must be put on the *democracy*, not on the *centralism*. The necessary equilibrium between them will be established on the basis of the new experience. (*Writings, 1936-37*, pp. 439-40)

Similarly, on September 18 he wrote Glotzer:

> The creation of an independent party with about two thousand members is a very important step forward. The inner regime in the party is of the greatest importance. It must be a regime of genuine democracy. I agree with you on the matter totally. Democracy presupposes not only a formal political but a pedagogical approach, to new members and to every workers' situation. It is correct that the leadership should be patient in its approach to the membership as the party should be in its approach to the working masses. (*Writings, 1936-37*, p. 441)

A week later, in another letter to Glotzer, Trotsky said, regarding the internal regime of the party, "The next period will be, in this respect, of great importance. We must give an example of genuine party democracy." (*Writings, 1936-37*, p. 445)

In October, Trotsky spelled out more fully what he meant by "party democracy," again emphasizing the pedagogical aspect. In particular, Trotsky stressed the importance of patience and a correct tone on the part of the leadership towards the rank and file. In those lines he provided one of the fullest definitions of "party democracy" that he ever gave, transcending the immediate needs of the party:

> What is party democracy?
>
> **a.** The strictest observance of the party statutes by the leading bodies (regular conventions, necessary period of discussion, right of the minority to express its opinions in the party meetings and in the press).
>
> **b.** A patient, friendly, to a certain point pedagogical attitude on the part of the central committee and its members toward the rank and file, including the objectors and the discontented, because it is not a great merit to be satisfied "with anybody who is satisfied with me." When Lenin asked for the expulsion of Ordzhonikidze from the party (1923), he said very correctly that the discontented party member has the right to be turbulent, but not a member of the central committee. Methods of psychological "terrorism," including a haughty or sarcastic manner of answering or treating every objection, criticism, or doubt—it is, namely, this journalistic or "intellectualistic" manner which is insufferable to workers and condemns them to silence.
>
> **c.** The solely formal object of the democratic rules as indicated under (a) and the solely negative measures—not to terrorize, not to ridicule—under (b) are not sufficient. The central committee as well as every local committee must be in permanent, active, and informal contact with the rank and file, especially when a new slogan or a new campaign is in preparation or when it is necessary to verify the results of an accomplished campaign. Not every member of the central committee is capable of such an informal contact, and not every member has the time for this or the occasion, which depends not only upon goodwill and a particular psychology but also upon the profession and the corresponding milieu. In the composition of the central committee it is necessary to have not only good organizers and good speakers, writers, administrators, but also people closely connected with the rank and file, organically representative of them. (*Writings, 1936-37*, pp. 476-77)

In a communication a few days later, Trotsky returned to the importance of "patience" in a party leadership:

> It is absolutely necessary to have the confidence of the rank and file. I mentioned the most important condition of this confidence—a good policy. The policy must be prepared with the understanding of the rank and file. It occurs often that the leadership, which sees a situation very well and has a very correct decision, imposes on the organization some imperative action, pushed by impatience, because the leadership feels that if we now begin a discussion of one

or two months, we will lose precious time. It may be a correct idea, but by gaining here a month I may lose a year, because the rank and file regards this change and speed with astonishment; and if success of the policy should be lacking, then the rank and file says, "The leadership was wrong; it bears the responsibility." And thus I lose a year to repair the results of my impatience.

That's why it is important, especially for a young organization, not to be impatient and to prepare for every new decision. First of all it is important to observe very strictly the statutes of the organization—regular meetings of the rank and file, discussions before conventions, regular conventions and the right of the minority to express its opinion (there should be a comradely attitude and not threats of expulsion). You know that was never, *never* done in the old [Russian] party. Expulsion of a comrade was a tragic event, and was done only for moral reasons and not because of a critical attitude. We had some comrades in opposition after the revolution. We had comrades who became specialists in criticism, not in principled matters but in minor ones. There was Stukhov, an intelligent man and a courageous one, as well as witty, and at every party meeting he found something to say, prefacing with a joke, and he had applause. Imagine during the civil war—there were many things to object to in the leadership, and he took advantage of it. But nobody proposed to expel him, but from time to time we explained to the members, and he began to lose his audience, and after a while Stukhov became a ridiculous figure.

He was one from the top of the party. In every body there were such Stukhovs. It was not a question of Stukhov but of the education of the party membership, an education that rejects unhealthy criticism, opposition only for the sake of opposition. I believe it is absolutely necessary also for the leadership to be very patient, to listen very attentively, very reasonably to criticism. (*Writings, 1936-37,* pp. 485-86)

Trotsky viewed the task of the proletarianization of the SWP as closely linked with the question of party democracy. Trotsky observed that the "predominance in the organization of intellectuals is inevitable in the first period of the development of the organization." But at the same time this had its negative consequences. In an organization predominantly composed of intellectuals "party life is just a period of discussion." And "it is at the same time a big handicap to the political education of the more gifted workers." (*Writings, 1936-37,* p. 475)

Trotsky proposed several measures to deal with these problems. First, he saw the need "to change the social composition of the organization—make it a workers organization." (*Writings, 1935-36,* p. 486) Second, he argued that it was "absolutely necessary at the next convention to introduce in the local and central committees as many workers as possible." He explained:

> The difficulty is that in every organization there are traditional committee members and that different secondary, factional, and personal considerations play too great a role in the composition of the list of candidates. The task is to break with routine, which is the beginning of bureaucratism; to convince the organization and especially its leading stratum (which is more difficult) of the necessity of a systematic renewal of the composition of all the leading bodies of the party. Naturally, the renewal can never be complete; a nucleus selected by the whole experience of the past is necessary in order to preserve the continuity of the party's politics. (*Writings, 1936-37*, p. 476)

And, third, he proposed an "orientation of the whole party toward factory work." Specifically, he suggested that the party "build up help commissions [composed of non-worker members] for oral and literary action in connection with our comrades in the union." (*Writings, 1936-37*, p. 489) Besides assisting the training of worker members and reorienting the party toward action, Trotsky believed these measures would improve the quality of democracy in the party. He thought that a more proletarian leadership, more oriented toward work in the factories, would be more responsive and sympathetic to the workers in the party. Trotsky pointed out: "…every functionary must be attentive to what the worker faces and what he needs. Many intellectuals and half-intellectuals terrorize the workers by some abstract generalities and paralyze the will toward activity. A functionary of a revolutionary party should have in the first place a good ear, and only in the second place a good tongue." (*Writings, 1936-37*, p. 490)

A larger proletarian composition and an orientation of the whole party to factory work would reduce the "terrorization" of worker members by intellectuals: "If we seriously established such a general orientation and if we verified the practical results every week, we would avoid a great danger: namely, that the intellectuals and white-collar workers might suppress the worker minority, condemn it to silence, transform the party into a very intelligent discussion club but absolutely not habitable for workers." (*Writings, 1936-37*, p. 490)

Trotsky was also concerned that steps be taken to overcome past differences. In this regard, he advised a conciliatory approach by the leaders of the former majority in dealing with the former minority:

Don't you believe that some concrete and sincere step could be made by the leaders of the former majority in order to eliminate the psychological remnants of the old struggle? What could this step be? In the first place, an open discussion in the committee with the most representative comrades of the former minority: Have we any principled difference with you? What are your organizational, or practical, or personal objections? Now, at the beginning of a great new chapter in the life of the party, we on our own part are absolutely ready to eliminate all the hindrances to close and harmonious cooperation. We are ready, for example, to eliminate anything resembling a factional caucus in the central committee. You find that the party regime is not sufficiently democratic? We are absolutely ready to accept every practical suggestion in order to eliminate any bureaucratic tendency and amplify the general party democracy, and so on. Such a discussion should be conducted without official procedure; that is, without concern for formulation in the minutes, etc. If the first discussion of such kind reveals itself as more or less promising, it could be repeated during the convention, especially with the consent of the members of the new National Committee.

The initiative should issue from the "majority," which only by general goodwill can disarm the minority. Let us imagine that some of the minority representatives, in spite of the best will on your part, continue their factional position. But the question is: Who will win by such a march of events? Not the factionalists surely. They will isolate themselves from their own closest friends. For the inner education and cohesion of the central committee, such a sincere attempt to reestablish the full mutual confidence could have only the best influence. (*Writings, 1936-37*, pp. 477-78)

Although his major emphasis in this period was on democracy, Trotsky simultaneously advised the former minority leader Glotzer that this must be tempered with a sense of responsibility. When Glotzer objected to the party regime, Trotsky advised him to be patient:

But there are methods of fighting for party democracy which are very dangerous to this aim. The present leadership—I mean *all* its members—is not an accidental one: it is a result of a selection, of a long period of struggle. In three to five years, new experiences can induce important changes in the composition and in the mentality of the leadership. But trying to change the leadership by some too-impatient, too-sharp measures can be fatal, and I can't conceal my impression that there are some disquieting symptoms in your letter. (*Writings, 1936-37*, p. 441)

It was particularly important in the upcoming convention to keep in mind that the majority of the membership had an entirely different organizational education than that of the Trotskyists:

> You will have, I assume, the greater half of the party composed of new elements. They agree with you on the principles but lack concrete experience in applying these principles. Their organizational education is totally different from yours. That is why your objections and arguments can assume in their heads a totally different meaning. Let us take, for example, the question whether it was or was not reasonable to enter the Socialist Party. For the "natives" the question does not exist at all. Your entry into the SP helped them to find the genuine, revolutionary road, and they will be at a loss even to understand the clash of opinions among their new leaders on this question. I will not say that therefore the question cannot be posed in the discussion but it is absolutely necessary to consider the new milieu and to observe the necessary proportions. (*Writings, 1936-37*, p. 443)

For this reason, Trotsky urged the "old guard" to:

> ...make every effort—naturally, not at the expense of principles—to present to the party unanimous drafts, or at least reduce the differences to concrete amendments to the common text and not to present opposing drafts and force the party to choose between them. These suggestions presume, naturally, insofar as I can judge, that irreconcilable differences do not exist now in the party, and even less in the leadership.... Democracy doesn't signify nonchalance and carelessness. And every outbreak of a sharp clash in the 'old guard' at this period would become inevitably prejudicial to party democracy and to the party as such. It is, naturally, not a question of forbidding discussion, or a "gag law" in our own party. It is only a reminder that the character of the discussion must be controlled by a sense of responsibility. (*Writings, 1936-37*, p. 445)

Preconvention discussion preparatory for the founding convention of the SWP opened in the autumn of 1937. A number of important differences, including on what attitude to take towards the Soviet Union in a war and on organizational questions, immediately emerged. A minority in what was to become the SWP argued that the Soviet Union was not a workers state. Some of those holding this view further rejected any defense of the Soviet Union in time of war. On the other hand, Burnham and Carter, who believed that the Soviet Union was neither a workers nor a bourgeois state, described their position as "defensist" with regard to the USSR. (That is, they still agreed with the majority that the USSR should be defended in any conflicts with capitalist countries.) But they defended the "right" of defeatists to remain in the party and carry on defeatist propaganda. Also, those holding minority views sharply criticized the "lack of democracy" and the "domineering of the 'leaders'" of the incipient SWP. Trotsky participated in the discussion through letters and contributions to the discussion bulletins. Writing to Burnham and Carter, he evaluated their focus on the "rights" of defeatists as "totally abstract, it seems to me, and at any rate not timely." (*Writings, 1937-38*, p. 85) Their error was in giving greater significance to the organizational question when the central issue was the need for the defense of the USSR in war. Trotsky warned that a mistaken position on that political question would have far more disastrous consequences than organizational errors. And he further warned that Burnham's and Carter's juridical defense of defeatists only strengthened the defeatists' false political position. Trotsky was not advocating an immediate organizational break with the defeatists. Rather, he placed primary emphasis on convincing them politically:

> "That means that you stand for an immediate organizational break with the defeatists?" you ask me. No, I reply. I stand for an immediate political break with defeatism. This is the first and chief problem. At the same time I favor taking all necessary measures in order to facilitate for the present defeatists their full assimilation into the party. We should give them the necessary time to think over the question seriously. Some of them will undoubtedly and very quickly renounce their point of view, which is in essence anti-Marxian. But others, on the contrary, will make out of their ultra-left mistake an everlasting platform. Of course, with the latter a break will prove inevitable. The whole course of the world workers' movement, beginning with July 1914, demonstrates that defeatists and defensists cannot remain in the same party, if the concept of a party has in general any sort of sense. The basic task of the present discussion consists in demonstrating the full political incompatibility of defeatism in relation to the USSR with membership in a revolutionary proletarian party. Only such an energetic—a Marxist and not a lawyer's—campaign against defeatism is capable of compelling the better part of the defeatists to reexamine their viewpoint. (*Writings, 1937-38*, pp. 85-6)

But at the same time, this did not give the minority members a license to disrupt the work of the majority:

> It is true that democracy presupposes likewise an attentive and patient attitude on the part of the majority toward the minority (so far as such a "patient" attitude is authorized by the course of the events themselves and so far as it is justified by the conduct of the

minority). But party democracy does not at all signify transforming the party into an arena for the free exercises of sectarians, blunderers, or aspiring individualists. Party democracy does not signify the right of the minority to upset the work of the majority. A revolutionary party is not a debating club but a militant organization. (*Writings, 1937-38*, p. 86)

Trotsky agreed with Burnham's view that in political questions it was impossible for a party to always have a perfect Bolshevik position. But, arguing against Burnham, Trotsky applied the same approach to questions of party organization. He wrote: "I agree with you...that organizational practice follows from general politics only in the *last instance*. In other words, that it has, within certain limits, an independent importance; that it can, consequently, influence for good or for bad the general policy." But Trotsky went on to disagree that political questions and organizational questions could be put "on the same plane." The political questions, he insisted, were of primary importance. He explained:

> You can object to my position with words from your letters; namely, that you are now "finishing up [an organizational] foundation which will determine the character of the building. A slight mistake now means disaster later on." But here is precisely the weakest point of your position. You reject, and rightly, the assertion that the "slightest deviation from Bolshevism involves necessarily a break from all of Bolshevism." But you repeat on the next page absolutely the same assertion only in relation to the organizational question. You wish with one stroke to provide a perfect foundation for party-building, and this aim dominates you with such power that you are ready to renounce not only a "perfect" Marxist policy but even a common fight in order to approach such a policy upon one of the most important questions of this historical period. (*Writings, 1937-38*, pp. 105-06)

Trotsky developed this latter point at length in a letter to the editors of the *Socialist Appeal*, regarding complaints from minority members about the lack of democracy in the organization. In doing so, Trotsky stressed that the working out of a correct balance of democracy and centralism was an ongoing process that always flowed from a correct policy:

> Neither do I think that I can give such a formula on democratic centralism that "once and for all" would eliminate misunderstandings and false interpretations. A party is an active organism. It develops in the struggle with outside obstacles and inner contradictions. The malignant decomposition of the Second and Third Internationals, under these severe conditions of the imperialist epoch, creates for the

Fourth International difficulties unprecedented in history. One cannot overcome them with some sort of magic formula. The regime of a party does not fall ready-made from the sky but is formed gradually in the struggle. A political line predominates over the regime. First of all, it is necessary to define strategic problems and tactical methods correctly in order to solve them. The organizational forms should correspond to the strategy and the tactic. Only a correct policy can guarantee a healthy party regime. This, it is understood, does not mean that the development of the party does not raise organizational problems as such. But it means that the formula for democratic centralism must inevitably find a different expression in the parties of different countries and in different stages of development of one and the same party. (*Writings, 1937-38*, pp. 89-90)

Trotsky traced the current dissatisfaction of the minority with the regime to the simple fact that they were a minority:

Sometimes, to judge by the tones of the letters, i.e., in the main instance by the formlessness of the grievances, it seems to be that the complainers are simply dissatisfied with the fact that in spite of the existing democracy, they prove to be in a tiny minority. Through my own experience I know that this is unpleasant. But wherein is there any violation of democracy? (*Writings, 1937-38*, p. 89)

He implied that some of them might simply be burned out politically and looking for scapegoats and panaceas: "Instead of seriously analyzing political questions in essence, such individuals seek panaceas, on every occasion complain about the 'regime,' demand wonders from the leadership, or try to muffle their inner skepticism by ultraleft prattling." (*Writings, 1937-38*, p. 91)

The minority was overwhelmingly defeated at the convention. But the same issues were to surface again two years later.

In late 1938 Trotsky had occasion to return to a number of the points he had made a year earlier during preparations for the founding of the SWP. When the left wing of the SP was expelled in 1937, a majority of the youth group of the SP—the Young Peoples Socialist League (YPSL)—supported the Trotskyists. In 1938 the YPSL shifted its affiliation to the new SWP. Nathan Gould, the national secretary of the YPSL, visited Trotsky in November, shortly before the first YPSL convention after its re-affiliation. In their discussion, Trotsky offered his views on the organizational norms of the youth group. As in the case of the SWP, he stressed the importance of democracy in the organization:

I believe democracy is very important in the organization. Why? Because democracy is perishing everywhere in the States, in the

trade unions, in the old revolutionary parties. Only we can permit
genuine honest democracy so that a young worker, a young student
can feel he has the possibility of expressing his opinion openly
without being immediately subjected to persecution. Ironical state-
ments from someone in authority is also persecution. We can at-
tract new members to the youth as to the party only by genuine
intelligent democracy. Everybody is tired of the lack of democracy.
(*Writings, 1938-39*, p. 121)

Again, Trotsky argued that an emphasis on democracy was necessitated
by the fact that the majority of members had no previous experience in a
democratic centralist organization:

> We can fail now in two directions. One in the direction of centraliza-
> tion; the other in the direction of democracy. I believe now we should
> exaggerate the democracy and be very, very patient with centralism in
> this transitional time. We must educate these people to understand
> the necessity of centralism. I am not sure that these losses were not to
> a certain degree due to the centralist impatience or lack of indulgence
> toward elements who had had no experience at all, who have had
> only the bad experience of the Socialist Party, who would breathe
> freely and who don't know themselves what they wish. They answer,
> "Now you say you will strangle us by genuine revolutionary Bolshe-
> vik methods." He is afraid and he says, "No, I will get out of the party."
> No, I am for democracy which can form the base for centralism, but
> centralism in a vacuum cannot create a democracy, it can only de-
> stroy what exists. (*Writings, 1938-39*, pp. 122-123)

Trotsky also saw the question of democracy as closely connected to the
relation between the party and the youth organization. He urged that the
party not maintain too tight a formal control over the youth. Rather, it
should work to gradually educate the youth by convincing them with its
arguments and by its example.

Trotsky wrote:

> It is clear that the youth cannot replace the party or duplicate the
> party. But that does not mean that we have the technical possibility
> of prohibiting the youth from trying to replace the party in every
> case where the youth think they find the party following a bad line.
> We cannot establish with one blow or with one resolution the au-
> thority of the party. We cannot create the authority for the party
> with one resolution. If the young comrades have two, three, five or
> ten experiences proving to them that the party is more wise, more
> experienced, then they will become more cautious in their opposi-
> tion to the party and more moderate in the forms of this opposition.
> Anyone who speaks in a tone of contempt to the party will immedi-

ately feel around himself a vacuum and irony of contempt and it will educate the people. But if we approach the young comrades with a general conception such as this: "Boys and girls, you acted very well against the Socialist Party because it was a bad party; but we are a good party. Don't forget it. You must not oppose us." How can you convince them with such a general conception? It is very dangerous. "You believe it is a good party, but we don't believe it!"

"Yes, we are against vanguardism insofar as it is directed against us."

Then they will answer, "You are bureaucrats, no more, no less." It is very dangerous. Theoretically it is correct like the question of discipline. Iron discipline, steel discipline, is absolutely necessary, but if the apparatus of the young party begins by demanding such iron discipline on the first day it can lose the party. It is necessary to educate confidence in the leadership of the party and the party in general because the leadership is only an expression of the party. (*Writings, 1938-39*, p. 122)

In writing about the relationship between the party and the youth, Trotsky offered some practical advice:

I do not know your plans about the new National Committee as you discussed it, but in order to make clear my opinion, I propose that if you have to choose a new [YPSL] National Committee of nineteen members do not introduce more than seven party members, less than one-half. The party members are party members. If they work in the youth we cannot give them the right to vote in the youth against the decisions of the National Committee [of the party]. Of course the National Committee of the party should not commit the mistake of adopting obligatory resolutions too early, especially concerning the youth, but if such a resolution is adopted with the full understanding of the party they must vote in the sense of the party. It is absolutely clear that it is their duty to convince the other twelve and to win them for this discussion. If they are defeated, the decision remains. The party cannot simply change a decision. (*Writings, 1938-39*, pp. 123-24)

e) 1939-40 factional dispute

The faction fight which erupted in the Socialist Workers Party in 1939-40 was the gravest crisis to confront the American Trotskyist movement since its inception. In that fight a large minority of the SWP leadership, reacting to new developments, attempted, in Trotsky's opinion, "to reject, disqualify and overthrow the theoretical foundation, the political principles and organizational methods of our movement." (*In Defense of Marxism*, p. 93)

A brilliant figure in the sizable minority current *was* someone who literally was a "bourgeois intellectual," James Burnham, who was beginning to question the validity of Marxism and to develop notions of "managerial society" that would lead him out of the socialist movement and make him famous when expounded in the 1941 best-seller *The Managerial Revolution*. (Burnham soon became a conservative anti-communist, ending up in the Central Intelligence Agency and as an editor of the influential right-wing magazine *National Review*.) The other key leader of the opposition was Max Shachtman, a seasoned Trotskyist who by no means shared Burnham's skepticism toward Marxism. Most of the oppositionists were closer to Shachtman's perspective. Trotsky believed, however, that Shachtman and others were adapting to de-radicalizing intellectuals like Burnham, and he called them "the petty-bourgeois opposition."

In the course of the discussion Trotsky helped to clarify the important issues involved and to lead the majority of the SWP in the defense of the dialectical methodology of Marxism and the Trotskyist movement's traditional view of the USSR. But just as important was his guidance to the party on organizational questions. With Trotsky's help the majority was able to defend the fundamental principles of democratic centralism, and to minimize the damage to the party from the heated factional fight and the ensuing split. Trotsky's contributions to this discussion provided the SWP then, and continue to provide us today, with a rich source for the study of the organizational principles of the revolutionary party.

In late August 1939 a peace pact was signed between Nazi Germany and the Soviet Union. World War II broke out. In September Soviet troops invaded Poland, and in November, Finland. These events all contributed to a rising tide of anti-Soviet hysteria in the United States. Trotsky felt that this, in turn, affected the large layer within a SWP at that time. Speaking for them and representing their moods were Max Shachtman, James Burnham, and Martin Abern, who formed a faction attempting to revise the traditional position of the party on the character of the USSR. Burnham maintained that the Soviet Union was neither a workers nor a bourgeois state. But he now rejected a defensist position. Shachtman claimed that he still supported the defense of the USSR in war, but showed his gravitation toward Burnham's position in his attempt to evade the question of the class nature of the Soviet Union, and even more in his characterization of the Soviet invasion of Poland as "imperialist." Finally, Abern and his followers claimed to support Trotsky's views, but ended up voting for *both* Shachtman's and the majority's resolutions at an NC plenum in September/

October. Trotsky believed that they were attempting to cover over their differences on the fundamental questions while voting together on "concrete" issues, forming an unprincipled alliance.

Trotsky also felt that part of the theoretical source for the errors of the minority on the Russian question could be traced to their abandonment of Marxist methodology. Again, Burnham took the lead by openly repudiating dialectics. Shachtman did not challenge the method of dialectical materialism in general, but argued that it was of no value in answering the specific political questions under discussion.

Against Shachtman, Trotsky repeatedly insisted that a correct position on the class nature of the Soviet Union was a necessary prerequisite for a correct position on the immediate political question posed by the outbreak of the war. Similarly, he argued that a dialectical methodology had a direct significance for the political tasks confronting the party. Against both Burnham and the rest of the minority moving toward Burnham's positions, Trotsky patiently reviewed the thinking behind the Marxist positions on both the character of the USSR and dialectical materialism.

But Trotsky further rejected what he saw as erroneous views of the minority on organizational questions. When the minority encountered firm resistance from the majority on political questions, it began to shift the discussion to organizational issues. In haste to change the party's position on the USSR, it demanded that the question be decided by a national referendum vote rather than by a convention. It accused the National Committee of "conservatism" in maintaining the old programmatic positions. It demanded that its views be published in the official party press, and, later, demanded the right to publish its own papers. It increasingly criticized the alleged repressiveness of the internal regime in the SWP.

Trotsky took up and rejected each of the minority's organizational demands. In doing so, he defended the centralist character of the party. First, Trotsky agreed with the majority's rejection of the demand for a referendum on the USSR, explaining at length how the referendum approach would undermine centralism:

> Whoever is in favor of a referendum recognizes by this that a party decision is simply an arithmetical total of local decisions, every one of the locals being inevitably restricted by its own forces and by its limited experience. Whoever is in favor of a referendum must be in favor of imperative mandates; that is, in favor of such a procedure that every local has the right to *compel* its representative at a party convention to vote in a definite manner. Whoever recognizes im-

perative mandates automatically denies the significance of conventions as the highest organ of the party. Instead of a convention it is sufficient to introduce a counting of local votes. The party as a centralized whole disappears. By accepting a referendum the influence of the most advanced locals and most experienced and farsighted comrades of the capital or industrial centers is substituted for the influence of the least experienced, backward sections, etc.

Naturally we are in favor of an all-sided examination and of voting upon every question by each party local, by each party cell. But at the same time every delegate chosen by a local must have the right to weigh all the arguments relating to the question in the convention and to vote as his political judgment demands of him. If he votes in the convention against the majority which delegated him, and if he is not able to convince his organization of his correctness after the convention, then the organization can subsequently deprive him of its political confidence. Such cases are inevitable. But they are incomparably a lesser evil than the system of referendums or imperative mandates which completely kill the party as a whole. (*In Defense of Marxism*, p. 33)

Against the accusation of "conservatism" Trotsky argued that "to defend the old programmatic decision until it is replaced by a new one is the elementary duty of the National Committee. I believe that such 'conservatism' is dictated by the self-preservation of the party itself." (*In Defense of Marxism*, p. 35) Trotsky recognized that it was permissible and under certain circumstances useful for the party press to print contributions from both sides of an internal debate. But he stressed that official publications had the duty to print the point of view of the party and the Fourth International.

He wrote:

> The *New International* and *Socialist Appeal* [the theoretical magazine and weekly newspaper of the SWP at this time] are not instruments of the discussion under the control of a special discussion committee, but rather instruments of the Party and its National Committee. In the discussion bulletin the opposition can ask for equal rights with the majority, but the official party publications have the duty to defend the point of view of the Party and the Fourth International until they are changed. A discussion on the pages of the official party publications can be conducted only within the limits established by the majority of the National Committee. It is so self-evident that arguments are not necessary. (*In Defense of Marxism*, p. 65)

In demanding the right to publish their own papers, the minority pointed to the precedent of the Bolshevik Party in the early years after the revolution. Trotsky explained the circumstances which made this necessary in the Soviet Union and which did not apply to the SWP in 1940:

> Shachtman finds, or better to say invents 'historical precedents.' In the Bolshevik Party the opposition had its own public papers, etc. He forgets only that the Party at that time had hundreds of thousands of members, that the discussion had as its task to reach these hundreds of thousands and to convince them. Under such conditions it was not easy to confine the discussion to internal circles. On the other hand the danger of the co-existence of the Party and the opposition papers was mitigated by the fact that the final decision depended upon hundreds of thousands of workers and not upon two small groups. The American Party has only a comparatively small number of members, the discussion was and is more than abundant. The demarcation lines seem to be firm enough at least for the next period. (*In Defense of Marxism*, p. 161)

Trotsky further denied the allegation that separate minority journals were permitted in the Bolshevik Party before and during World War I: "The resolution says: 'Minorities of the Bolshevik Party both before and during the First World War' had their own public political journals. What minorities? At what time? What journals? The leaders induce their followers into an error in order to camouflage their split intentions." (*In Defense of Marxism*, p. 163)

Trotsky explained that the entire organizational approach of the minority was mistaken:

> The organizational structure of the proletarian vanguard must be subordinated to the positive demands of the revolutionary fight and not to the negative guarantees against their degeneration. If the Party is not fit for the needs of the socialist revolution, it would degenerate in spite of the wisest juridicial stipulations. On the organizational field, Burnham shows a complete lack of revolutionary conception of the party. (*In Defense of Marxism*, p. 65)

Trotsky described two factors which he felt were responsible for the mistaken organizational views of the minority. First, he noted the tendency of the minority to substitute organizational questions when the incorrectness of its political questions had been made clear:

> Thus in two most important issues of the last period comrades dissatisfied with the 'regime' have had in my opinion a false political attitude. The regime must be an instrument for correct policy and not for false. When the incorrectness of their policy becomes clear, then its protagonists are often tempted to say that not this special issue is

decisive but the general regime. During the development of the Left Opposition and the Fourth International we opposed such substitutions hundreds of times. When Vereeken or Sneevliet or even Molinier were beaten on all their points of difference, they declared that the genuine trouble with the Fourth International is not this or that decision but the bad regime. (*In Defense of Marxism*, p. 35-6)

But, as in the political disagreements, Trotsky saw the deeper source of differences in what he viewed as the petty-bourgeois character of the opposition:

It is necessary to call things by their right names. Now that the positions of both factions in the struggle have become determined with complete clearness, it must be said that the minority of the National Committee is leading a typical petty-bourgeois tendency. Like any petty-bourgeois group inside the socialist movement, the present opposition is characterized by the following features: a disdainful attitude toward theory and an inclination toward eclecticism; disrespect for the tradition of their own organization; anxiety for personal 'independence' at the expense of anxiety for objective truth; nervousness instead of consistency; readiness to jump from one position to another; lack of understanding of revolutionary centralism and hostility toward it; and finally, inclination to substitute clique ties and personal relationships for party discipline. (*In Defense of Marxism*, p. 43)

Trotsky noted that it would be incorrect to think that the minority's shift to organizational questions was a simple maneuver:

No, the inner feelings of the opposition tell them, in truth, however confusedly, that the issue concerns not only the "Russian problem" but rather the entire approach to political problems in general, including also the methods of building the party. And this is in a certain sense correct.

We too have attempted above to prove that the issue concerns not only the Russian problem but even more the opposition's method of thought, which has its social roots. The opposition is under the sway of petty-bourgeois moods and tendencies. This is the essence of the whole matter. (*In Defense of Marxism*, p. 59)

The opposition's conception of the party, in Trotsky's opinion, revealed their petty-bourgeois obsession with discussion.

A worker spends his day at the factory. He has comparatively few hours left for the party. At the meetings he is interested in learning the most important things: the correct evaluation of the situation and the political conclusions. He values those leaders who do this in the clearest and most precise form and who keep in step with events. Petty-bourgeois, and especially declassed elements, divorced from the proletariat, vegetate in an artificial and shut-in environment. They have ample time to dabble in politics or its substitute. They pick out faults, exchange all sorts of tidbits and gossip concerning happenings among the party "tops." They always locate a leader who initiates them into all the 'secrets.' Discussion is their native element. No amount of democracy is ever enough for them. For their war of words they seek the fourth dimension. They become jittery, they revolve in a vicious circle, and they quench their thirst with salt water. Do you want to know the organizational program of the opposition? It consists of a mad hunt for the fourth dimension of party democracy. In practice this means burying politics beneath discussion; and burying centralism beneath the anarchy of the intellectual circles. When a few thousand workers join the party, they will call the petty-bourgeois anarchists severely to order. The sooner, the better. (*In Defense of Marxism*, p. 92)

And the "petty-bourgeois" character of the minority's views was evident in this search for an "ideal democracy" which would guarantee full freedom for the individual:

...you...seek an ideal party democracy which would secure forever and for everybody the possibility of saying and doing whatever popped into his head, and which would insure the party against bureaucratic degeneration. You overlook a trifle, namely, that the party is not an arena for the assertion of free individuality, but an instrument of the proletarian revolution; that only a victorious revolution is capable of preventing the degeneration not only of the party but of the proletariat itself and of modern civilization as a whole. You do not see that our American section is not sick from too much centralism—it is laughable even to talk about it—but from a monstrous abuse and distortion of democracy on the part of petty-bourgeois elements. This is at the root of the present crisis. (*In Defense of Marxism*, p. 92)

But it was not just their fear that their individual "rights" would be violated that led the opposition to propose an open discussion in the party press, and later, to demand the right to publish their own papers. Rather, Trotsky asserted, they wanted to be able to justify themselves in the eyes of such "independent radicals" as the writer Max Eastman and the professor Sidney Hook, who had once been close to Trotskyism but were now shifting to the right. Trotsky wrote:

What is then the source of their thirst for publicity? The explanation is very simple: they are impatient to justify themselves before the democratic public opinion, to shout to all the Eastmans, Hooks and the others that they, the opposition, are not so bad as we. This inner necessity must be especially imperative with Burnham. It is the same kind of inner capitulation which we observed in Zinoviev and Kamenev on the eve of the October Revolution and by many "internationalists" under the pressure of the patriotic war wave. (*In Defense of Marxism*, p. 66)

Finally, Trotsky focused on what he saw as the petty-bourgeois character of the Abern clique within the minority, which seemed to place personal ties above political principles and loyalty to the party. Trotsky wrote:

If we subtract everything accidental, personal and episodical, if we reduce the present groupings in struggle to their fundamental political types, then indubitably the struggle of comrade Abern against comrade Cannon has been the most consistent. In this struggle Abern represents a propagandistic group, petty-bourgeois in its social composition, united by old personal ties and having almost the character of a family. Cannon represents the proletarian party in process of formation. The historical right in this struggle— independent of what errors and mistakes might have been made— rests wholly on the side of Cannon.

When the representatives of the opposition raised the hue and cry that the "leadership is bankrupt," "the prognoses did not turn out to be correct," "the events caught us unawares," "it is necessary to change our slogans," all this without the slightest effort to think the questions through seriously, they appeared fundamentally as party defeatists. This deplorable attitude is explained by the irritation and fright of the old propagandistic circle before the new tasks and the new party relations. The sentimentality of personal ties does not want to yield to the sense of duty and discipline. The task that stands before the party is to break up the old clique ties and to dissolve the best elements of the propagandistic past in the proletarian party. It is necessary to develop such a spirit of party patriotism that nobody dare say: "The reality of the matter is not the Russian question but that we feel more easy and comfortable under Abern's leadership than under Cannon's."

I personally did not arrive at this conclusion yesterday. I happened to have expressed it tens and hundreds of times in conversations with members of Abern's group. I invariably emphasized the petty-bourgeois composition of this group. I insistently and repeatedly proposed to transfer from membership to candidacy such petty-bourgeois fellow-travellers as proved incapable of recruiting workers for the party. Private letters, conversations and admonitions as has been shown by subsequent events have not led to anything— people rarely learn from someone else's experience. The antagonism between the two party layers and the two periods of its development rose to the surface and took on the character of bitter factional struggle. Nothing remains but to give an opinion, clearly and definitely, to the American section and the whole International. "Friendship is friendship but duty is duty"—says a Russian proverb. (*In Defense of Marxism*, p. 61)

After it came to light that Abern had been selectively "leaking" confidential information of the National Committee and Political Committee to his own supporters around the country, Trotsky urged that steps be taken to prevent such acts by NC and PC members. (See *In Defense of Marxism*, pp. 163-64)

Although in his contributions to the discussion Trotsky was primarily concerned with combatting what he viewed as false and anti-Marxist positions of the minority, on several occasions he also offered organizational advice to the majority. Joseph Hansen and William F. Warde [George Novack] explain in their introduction to *In Defense of Marxism*,

> The majority endeavored to maintain unity, acting under the conviction that the unity of the revolutionary party and inculcation of party patriotism are among its most precious assets. The majority likewise had two objectives: (1) to keep wavering elements in the minority under the maximum influence of our program; (2) to prove conclusively to the other sections of the Fourth International that if matters come to a split the responsibility for the split rested wholly with the minority. (*In Defense of Marxism*, p. XIV)

In line with these objectives, Trotsky urged the majority to avoid a split, and should it eventually find itself in the minority, to act in accordance with party discipline. Trotsky was fully confident in the strength of the revolutionary program, and, consequently, in the possibility of rallying a decisive majority of SWP cadres to that program in the near future. He therefore warned against rigid or mechanistic organizational measures that would artificially "resolve" (but that would, in fact, cut across) this necessary educational process. He explained:

> …I believe that the implacable ideological fight should go parallel with very cautious and wise organizational tactics. You have not the slightest interest in a split, even if the opposition should become, accidentally, a majority at the next convention. You have not the slightest reasons to give the heterogeneous and unbalanced army of the opposition a pretext for a split. Even as an eventual minority, you should in my opinion remain disciplined and loyal towards the party as a whole. It is extremely important for the education in genuine

party patriotism, about the necessity of which Cannon wrote me one time very correctly. (*In Defense of Marxism*, p. 63)

To make a split more difficult, Trotsky suggested that the majority adopt a conciliatory attitude toward the minority. Specifically, it should reaffirm the existing rights of minority factions and should make an extraordinary gesture by prolonging the discussion and then providing a form for making the discussion public:

> But I wish to speak here about another more important question. Some of the leaders of the opposition are preparing a split; whereby they represent the opposition in the future as a persecuted minority. It is very characteristic of their state of mind. I believe we must answer them approximately as follows:
> "You are already afraid of our future repressions? We propose to you mutual guarantees for the future minority, independently of who might be this minority, you or we. These guarantees could be formulated in four points: (1) No prohibition of factions; (2) No other restrictions on factional activity than those dictated by the necessity for common action; (3) The official publications must represent, of course, the line established by the new convention; (4) The future minority can have, if it wishes, an internal bulletin destined for party members, or a common discussion bulletin with the majority."
> The continuation of discussion bulletins immediately after a long discussion and a convention is, of course, not a rule but an exception, a rather deplorable one. But we are not bureaucrats at all. We don't have immutable rules. We are dialecticians also in the organizational field. If we have in the party an important minority which is dissatisfied with the decisions of the convention, it is incomparably more preferable to legalize the discussion after the convention than to have a split.
> We can go, if necessary, even further and propose to them to publish, under the supervision of the new National Committee, special discussion symposiums, not only for party members, but for the public in general. We should go as far as possible in this respect in order to disarm their at least premature complaints and handicap them in provoking a split. (*In Defense of Marxism*, p. 101)

Even after the minority held its own national conference in February 1940, Trotsky continued to advise conciliation on the part of the majority. Even accepting Cannon's premise that a split was inevitable and that no more minority members could be won over, Trotsky argued, "We must do everything in order to convince also the other sections that the Majority exhausted all the possibilities in favor of unity." (*In Defense of Marxism*, p. 158)

Finally, just before the SWP convention, Trotsky proposed that if a split were avoided organizational concessions should be made to the minority:

> But in the case that the Minority makes a retreat, I permit myself to insist upon my previous propositions. The necessity of preserving the secrets of the discussions and decisions in the National Committee is a very important interest but not the only one and in the present situation not the most important. About 40 per cent of Party members believe Abern is the best organizer. If they remain inside the Party, you cannot help but give Abern the chance to show his superiority in organizational matters or to compromise himself....
>
> If the Opposition is wavering, it would be best to let them know in an informal way: We are ready to retain Shachtman as a member not only of the Political Committee but also of our editorial staff; we are even ready to include Abern in the Secretariat; we are willing to consider other combinations of the same kind; the only thing we cannot accept is the transformation of the Minority into an independent political factor. (*In Defense of Marxism*, pp. 163-64)

As it turned out, the minority was not "wavering." It split from the Socialist Workers Party in April 1940. The 1939-40 discussion in the SWP, however, had been a full and democratic one. Following Trotsky's advice, the majority had gone out of its way to make it possible for the minority to remain in the party. What's more, Trotsky's participation in the discussion had helped to clarify the important theoretical, political and organizational issues involved. Consequently, the exit of the opposition left the SWP and the Fourth International in some ways stronger than they had been before.

6. The Fourth International

> The very sequence of the Internationals has its own internal logic, which coincides with the historic rise of the proletariat. The First International advanced the scientific program of the proletarian revolution, but it fell because it lacked a mass base. The Second International dragged from the darkness, educated, and mobilized millions of workers, but in the decisive hour it found itself betrayed by the parliamentary and the trade union bureaucracy corrupted by rising capitalism. The Third International set for the first time the example of the victorious proletarian revolution, but it found itself ground between the millstones of the bureaucracy in the isolated soviet state and the reformist bureaucracy of the West. Today, under the conditions of decisive capitalist collapse, the Fourth International, standing upon the shoulders of its predecessors, enriched by the experience of their victories and defeats, will mobilize

the toilers of the Occident and the Orient for the victorious assault upon the strongholds of world capital. (*Writings, 1935-36*, pp. 27-8)

In this thumb-nail historical sketch, written in 1935, Trotsky indicated the world-historic importance of the Fourth International. Of course, the Fourth International (World Party of Socialist Revolution) had not been formally established at this time. But since 1930, an organized international network had existed. In 1933, the International Left Opposition had proclaimed the need for a Fourth International and adopted the interim name of the International Communist League. Although the founding conference of the Fourth International had to wait until September 1938, an international organization, composed of national sections and based on Bolshevik-Leninist political and organizational principles, had already existed for several years.

In 1932, Trotsky explained the reasons for such an international organization in a letter to Spanish comrades:

> Not to know...[national] peculiarities would of course be the greatest idiocy. But underneath them we must know how to discover the motivating forces of international developments and grasp the dependence of national peculiarities upon the world combination of forces. The tremendous advantage of Marxism and consequently of the Left Opposition consists precisely in this international manner of solving national problems and national peculiarities.
>
> For your young organization a particular task is carefully following the work of the other sections of the International Left Opposition in order always to do your work in conformity with the interests of the whole. Without international criteria, without regular international links, without control over the work of a national section, the formation of a true revolutionary proletarian organization is impossible in our epoch. (*The Spanish Revolution*, p. 173; also see *Writings, 1930*, pp 285-86 for a similar explanation.)

Yet the environment in which the Fourth International struggled to establish itself was far from hospitable. As Trotsky wrote in 1936 (all too prophetically, as it turned out):

> Not a single revolutionary grouping in world history has yet experienced such terrible pressure as the grouping of the Fourth International. The Communist Manifesto of Marx and Engels spoke of the forces of the "pope and the czar...French Radicals and German police" united against communism. From this list only the czar is now missing. But the Stalinist bureaucracy is a far more threatening and treacherous obstacle on the road of the world revolution than the autocratic czar once was. The Comintern covers a policy of social patri-

otism and Menshevism with the authority of the October Revolution and the banner of Lenin. [Trotsky is here referring to the Comintern's new "People's Front" policy, which, "as a coalition with the bourgeoisie, is a brake on the revolution and a safety valve for imperialism."] The world agency of the GPU is ready, hand-in-hand with the police of "friendly" imperialist countries, carrying on systematic work against the Fourth International. In the event of the outbreak of war, the united forces of imperialism and Stalinism will inflict upon the revolutionary internationalists immeasurably more furious persecutions than those which the generals of the Hohenzollerns together with the Social Democratic butchers inflicted in their time upon Luxemburg, Liebknecht, and their supporters. (*Writings, 1935-36*, pp. 338-39, 335)

Trotsky's response was free from passivity and despair:

The new parties and the new International must be built upon a new foundation: that is the key with which to solve all other tasks. The tempo and the time of the new revolutionary construction and its consummation depend, obviously, upon the general course of the class struggle, the future victories and defeats of the proletariat. Marxists, however, are not fatalists. They do not unload upon the "historical process" those very tasks which the historical process has posed before them. The initiative of a conscious minority, a scientific program, bold and ceaseless agitation in the name of clearly formulated aims, merciless criticism of all ambiguity—those are some of the most important factors for the victory of the proletariat. (*Writings, 1935-36*, p. 27)

As we have already seen, Trotsky insisted that "genuine unity of the International and of its national sections can be assured only upon the revolutionary Marxist foundation," and that "to remain silent about the principled conditions and guarantees for proletarian unity is to join in the chorus for broadcasting illusions, duping the workers, and preparing new catastrophes." The revolutionary program is primary. "How the new International will take form, through what stages it will pass, what final shape it will assume—this no one can foretell today.... But it is necessary to begin by proclaiming a *program* that meets the tasks of our epoch. On the basis of this program it is necessary to mobilize cothinkers, the pioneers of the new International. No other road is possible." (*Writings, 1935-36*, pp. 25, 159)

At the same time, Trotsky warned against sectarian abstentionism and doctrinaire rigidity, insisting "it is not enough to create a correct program. It is necessary for the working class to accept it. But the sectarian, in the nature of things, comes to a stop upon the first half of the task. Active intervention into the actual struggle of the masses of workers is supplanted for him by propagandistic abstractions of a Marxist program." Stressing the need to "do away with the vices of sectarianism and pedantic phrase-mongering in our own ranks," he explained:

> Fealty to the ideological banner is the indispensable and funda-
> mental quality of the genuine revolutionist. But woe to him who
> turns this "fealty" into doctrinaire stubbornness, into repetition of
> ready-made, once-and-for-all learned formulas. Genuine Marxist
> policy means carrying the ideas of the proletarian revolution to
> ever wider masses, through ever changing and ever new and fre-
> quently unexpected combinations of historic conditions. (*Writings,
> 1935-36*, pp. 152-53; *Writings, 1937-38*, p. 384)

In Trotsky's opinion, "every real mass movement freshens the atmosphere like a storm, and at the same time destroys every kind of political fic-
tion and ambiguity." A revolutionary program is inseparable from political
action, which it helps to develop—and which also helps develop it.

> The relation between theory and practice bears not a one-sided but
> a two-sided—that is, dialectical—character. We are sufficiently
> equipped theoretically for action; at any rate much better than any
> other organization. Our action will push our theoretical work for-
> ward, will arouse and attract new theoreticians, etc. The Fourth In-
> ternational will never spring from our hands ready made like
> Minerva from the head of Jupiter. It will grow and develop in the-
> ory as well as in action.

Implicit in a *genuine* commitment to the revolutionary program is a genuine
commitment to involvement in the ongoing struggles of the workers and the
oppressed. (*Writings, 1935-36*, p. 336; *Writings, 1937-38*, pp. 346-47)

Trotsky saw the two most serious problems within the Fourth International as being a pull toward sectarianism on the one hand and toward
centrism on the other—each demonstrating a failure to grasp the revolutionary dialectic between theory and practice:

> How many times have we met a smug centrist who reckons himself
> a "realist" merely because he sets out to swim without any ideologi-
> cal baggage whatever and is tossed by every vagrant current. He is
> unable to understand that principles are not dead ballast but a life
> line for a revolutionary swimmer. The sectarian, on the other hand,
> generally does not want to go swimming at all, in order not to wet
> his principles. He sits on the shore and reads lectures on morality to
> the flood of the class struggle. But sometimes a desperate sectarian

leaps headlong into the water, seizes hold of the centrist and helps him drown. So it was; so it will be. (*Writings, 1935-36*, p. 154)

Trotsky was determined, as he fought to establish the Fourth International, to triumph over these twin dangers within the ranks of the new International. "We always analyze the living stream and adapt ourselves to every new situation without losing our identity," Trotsky wrote. "Therein lies the whole secret of revolutionary success." (*Writings, 1934-35*, p. 205) The organizational method for achieving this was democratic centralism. This, of course, assumes a basic commitment to the program and organizational principles of the Fourth International on the part of its national sections. And it was precisely on this question that certain sections were ambivalent. Trotsky explained:

> We must devote the greatest attention to all the vacillating and immature working class groupings that are developing in our direction. But we cannot make principled concessions to sectarian-centrist leaders who want to recognize neither our international organization nor our discipline.
>
> "That means you want a monolithic International?" someone will say in holy fear. No, least of all that, I will reply calmly to this suspicion. The entire history of the Fourth International and each of its sections shows a constant, uninterrupted, and free struggle of points of view and tendencies. But as our experience testifies, this struggle retains a sane character only when its participants consider themselves members of one and the same national and international organization which has its program and its constitution. We can, on the other hand, carry on a comradely discussion with groups who stand outside of our organization. But as the experience with Sneevliet [of the Dutch section] and Vereecken [of the Belgian section] indicates, the discussion inevitably assumes a poisoned character when some leaders stand with one foot in our organization, the other—outside of it. To allow the development of such a regime would be suicidal. (*Writings, 1937-38*, pp. 347-48)

As Trotsky wrote in a frank letter to Sneevliet: "If you don't accept common rules for collaboration and active solidarity; if you renounce participating normally, like every other section, in the International [Founding] Conference; if you will continue with the totally ambiguous attitude—in words with the Fourth International, in deeds against it—then it is better to undergo an open and honest split." On the other hand, Trotsky was far from being rigid on the question of relationships between national sections and the Fourth International. "Any attempt to prescribe an identical course for all countries would be fatal," he asserted.

> We cannot make any claim to leading our national sections directly
> from a center, even if this center were much more united than it is
> at present. Within the bounds of the united program and the com-
> mon political line, every section must necessarily lay claim to a cer-
> tain elbow room in which to act. (*Writings, 1937-38*, p. 83; *Writings,
> 1935-36*, pp. 25, 366)

Nor was there any rigidity in Trotsky's views regarding political deviations within national sections. Corresponding with an American comrade,
he wrote:

> You quote comrades who say that "the slightest deviation from Bol-
> shevism involves a break from all of Bolshevism." Such an assertion
> is absurd. A living party can approach a relatively correct policy
> only by successive approximations; that is, by [successive] devia-
> tions to the right and to the left. The same is true for every party
> member, individually…. The vigor of the party and the skill of its
> leadership are tested by their capacity to assimilate the partial devi-
> ations in time and not permit them to lead to a complete break
> with Marxism. (*Writings, 1937-38*, p. 105)

This process of achieving "a relatively correct policy by successive ap-
proximations" is realized through democratic centralism. Trotsky described the process in this way:

> The revolutionary party presents a definite program and definite
> tactics. This placed definite and very distinct limits on the internal
> struggle of tendencies and groupings in advance…The very fact of
> membership in the Fourth International cannot but be contingent
> upon observance of a certain body of restrictions which reflect all
> the experiences of previous working class movements. But al-
> though the limits on the internal ideological struggle are thus es-
> tablished in advance, the struggle itself, carried on within the limits
> of general principles, is not at all denied. It is inevitable; and when
> it is within the prescribed limits it is fruitful. It is not discussion, of
> course, that gives the life of the party its fundamental content, but
> struggle…. But where discussion is rooted in the common struggle,
> where it puts the struggle under a critical light and prepares for its
> new stages—there, discussion is an element that is indispensable
> for development. (*Writings, 1935-36*, pp. 187-88)

Asked how far can factions develop with safety to the party, Trotsky responded:

> Generally it is best to let petty-bourgeois tendencies express them-
> selves fully so that they may expose themselves. If there are no such
> tendencies, if the membership is fairly homogeneous, there will be

only temporary groupings—unless the leadership is incorrect. And this will be shown best in practice. So, when a difference occurs, a discussion should take place, a vote be taken, and a majority line adopted. There must be no discrimination against the minority; any personal animosity will compromise not them but the leadership. Real leadership will be loyal and friendly to the disciplined minority…. Organizational measures should be resorted to only in extreme cases. Discipline is built by education, not only by statutes. It was the flexible life within it which allowed the Bolshevik Party to build its discipline. (*Writings, 1935-36*, pp. 204-05)

Trotsky wrote: "I am for democracy which can form the base for centralism, but centralism in a vacuum cannot create a democracy, it can only destroy what exists." (*Writings, 1938-39*, p. 123) Yet his belief in the necessity of centralism was firm. This is revealed, for example, in Trotsky's 1938 comments about a leader of the Mexican section who was guilty of "sectarian intrigue" and "political passivity" and with "ignoring our International in the name of solidarity with all the centrist and ultraleft cliques." Trotsky charged:

He is demanding that the International guarantee complete freedom for his individuality. He completely forgets about *centralism*. But for the revolutionist, democracy is only one element of organization; the other no less important element is centralism, since without centralism revolutionary activity is impossible. *Democracy guarantees freedom to discuss: centralism guarantees unity in action.*

As he had stressed more than once: "The Fourth International will not allow anyone—of this we have no doubt—to take lightly either our principles or our discipline." (*Writings, 1938-39*, pp. 145, 148, 143; *Writings, 1935-36*, p. 184)

A genuine commitment to the revolutionary program, to organizational centralism and to internal democracy—those were the pillars of the Fourth International, written into *The Transitional Program*:

The Fourth International…uncompromisingly gives battle to all political groupings tied to the apron-strings of the bourgeoisie. Its task—the abolition of capitalism's domination. Its aim—socialism. Its method—the proletarian revolution.

Without inner democracy—no revolutionary education. Without discipline—no revolutionary action. The inner structure of the Fourth International is based on the principles of democratic centralism: full freedom in discussion, complete unity in action. (*The Transitional Program for Socialist Revolution*, p. 111)

CONCLUSION

In his 1937 pamphlet *Stalinism and Bolshevism*, Trotsky summarized the
necessity of a revolutionary vanguard party in this way:

> The proletariat can take power only through its vanguard. In itself
> the necessity for state power arises from an insufficient cultural
> level of the masses and their heterogeneity. In the revolutionary
> vanguard, organized in a party, is crystallized the aspiration of the
> masses to obtain their freedom. Without the class's support of the
> vanguard, there can be no talk of the conquest of power. In this
> sense the proletarian revolution and dictatorship are the work of
> the whole class, but only under the leadership of the vanguard. The
> soviets [i.e., democratic councils] are only the organized form of
> the tie between the vanguard and the class. A revolutionary content
> can be given to this form only by the party. This is proved by the
> positive experience of the October Revolution [in Russia] and by
> the negative experience of other countries (Germany, Austria, fi-
> nally Spain). No one has either shown in practice or tried to explain
> articulately on paper how the proletariat can seize power without
> the political leadership of the party that knows what it wants.
> (*Writings, 1936-37*, p. 426)

The bedrock of the organizational principles of the revolutionary party
is the revolutionary program that flows from the doctrines of Marxism.
"One of the most outstanding features of Bolshevism," Trotsky wrote, "has
been its severe, exacting, even quarrelsome attitude toward questions of
doctrine." (*Writings, 1936-37*, p. 427)

He elaborated:

> The Bolshevik Party has shown in action a combination of the highest revolutionary audacity and political realism. It has established for the first time the only relation between vanguard and class that can assure victory. It has proved by experience that the alliance between the proletariat and the oppressed masses of the rural and urban petty bourgeoisie is possible only through the political defeat of the traditional petty-bourgeois parties. The Bolshevik Party has shown the entire world how to carry out armed insurrection and the seizure of power....
>
> But this is not all. The Bolshevik Party was able to carry on its magnificent 'practical' work only because it illuminated all its steps with theory. Bolshevism did not create this theory: it was furnished by Marxism. But Marxism is the theory of movement, not of stagnation. Only events on a tremendous historical scale could enrich the theory itself. Bolshevism brought an invaluable contribution to Marxism in its analysis of the imperialist epoch as an epoch of wars and revolutions; of bourgeois democracy in the era of decaying capitalism; of the correlation between the general strike and the insurrection; of the role of party, soviets, and trade unions in the period of proletarian revolution; in its theory of the Soviet state, of the economy of transition of fascism and Bonapartism in the epoch of capitalist decline; finally in its analysis of the degeneration of both the Bolshevik Party itself and of the Soviet state. (*Writings, 1936-37*, pp. 430-31)

Here, of course, Trotsky is including his own contributions and those of the Fourth International. "Only the founders of the Fourth International, who have made the whole tradition of Marx and Lenin their own, take a serious attitude toward theory," he wrote.

> Philistines may jeer that twenty years after the October victory the revolutionaries are again thrown back to modest propagandist preparation.... [But] the burning historical need for revolutionary leadership promises to the Fourth International an exceptionally rapid tempo of growth. The greatest guarantee of its further success lies in the fact that it has not arisen apart from the large historic road, but is an organic outgrowth of Bolshevism. (*Writings, 1936-37*, p. 431)

We have seen that continuity with the revolutionary traditions of Bolshevism has meant a thoroughgoing rejection of Social Democratic and Stalinist politics—in the realm of both programmatic and organizational principles. Inseparable from the revolutionary program is a commitment to mass action against capitalist injustice, to the living class struggle, to the movement of the working class:

The *Communist Manifesto* of Marx and Engels, directly aimed
against all types of utopian-sectarian socialism, forcefully points
out that Communists *do not* oppose themselves to the actual workers' movements but participate in them as a vanguard. At the same
time the *Manifesto* was the program of a *new party*, national and
international. The sectarian is content with a program, as a recipe
for salvation. The centrist guides himself by the famous (essentially
meaningless) formula of Edward Bernstein: "the movement is
everything; the final goal—nothing." The Marxist draws his scientific program from the movement taken as a whole, in order then to
apply this program to every concrete stage of the movement. (*Writings, 1935-36*, p. 159)

Trotsky stressed time and again: "The International is first of all a program, and a system of *strategic, tactical, and organizational* methods that
flow from it." (*Writings, 1935-36*, p. 147) The key organizational method of
Bolshevism, and thus of the Fourth International, is democratic centralism: full freedom of discussion, complete unity in action. The function of
democratic centralism is to make the revolutionary program a living reality: to develop fully (as activists, organizers and critical-minded Marxists)
increasing numbers of revolutionary cadres, to join them together as an effective political force, to enable them to determine collectively how the revolutionary program shall be applied in the ongoing struggles of the
workers and the oppressed.

The very perspective of building such a Bolshevik-Leninist party sug-
gests a strategy for socialist revolution, one which places immense responsibilities on the party leadership and rank-and-file. All must absorb, defend
and utilize—thereby renewing—the rich heritage of organizational principles which were embodied in Trotsky's own political practice.

WORKS CITED

E. H. Carr, *The Bolshevik Revolution, 1917-1923*, 3 vols. Baltimore: Penguin Books, 1966.

V. I. Lenin, *Selected Works*, 3 vols. New York: International Publishers, 1967.

V. I. Lenin and Leon Trotsky, *Lenin's Fight Against Stalinism*. New York: Pathfinder Press, 1975.

J. V. Stalin, *Problems of Leninism*. Peking: Foreign Languages Press, 1976.

Works by Leon Trotsky

The Challenge of the Left Opposition, 1923-25. New York: Pathfinder Press, 1975.

The Challenge of the Left Opposition, 1926-27. New York: Pathfinder Press, 1980.

The Challenge of the Left Opposition, 1928-29. New York: Pathfinder Press, 1981.

The Crisis of the French Section, 1935-36. New York: Pathfinder Press, 1977.

The History of the Russian Revolution. New York: Monad Press, 1980.

In Defense of Marxism. New York: Pathfinder Press, 1970.

My Life. New York: Pathfinder Press, 1970.

1905. New York: Vintage Books, 1972.

The Revolution Betrayed. New York: Pathfinder Press, 1970.

The Spanish Revolution, 1931-39. New York: Pathfinder Press, 1973.

The Stalin School of Falsification. New York: Pathfinder Press, 1971.

The Struggle Against Fascism in Germany. New York: Pathfinder Press, 1971.

The Third International After Lenin. New York: Pathfinder Press, 1970.

The Transitional Program for Socialist Revolution, 2nd Edition. New York: Pathfinder Press, 1974.

The War and the International. Ceylon: Young Socialist Publications, 1971.

Writings of Leon Trotsky, 1929-40, 14 volumes, including supplements. New York: Pathfinder Press, 1973-79.

CPSIA information can be obtained
at www.ICGtesting.com
Printed in the USA
JSHW020313250322
24242JS00006B/13

9 781608 463961